ECONOMIC MENACES&THE INTRINSIC VALUES OF THE FORMAL&INFORMAL EDUCATION AS REMEDY

TOPE ADENIJI

DEDICATION

The book is dedicated to the Almighty and sufficient God.

Also, it is strictly dedicated to my loving, caring and an angel that has contributed immensely to my making and being, Late Evangelist Mrs Mary Aderonke Adeniji, my dearest Mother. Your remembrance lives on in the contents of my philosophy to the humanity concern.

Teachers of all empirical studies are not exempted.

TABLE OF CONTENTS

TITTLE PAGE	1
DEDICATION	2
TABLE OF CONTENTS	3
ACKNOWLEDEMENT	4-7
INTRODUCTION	8-13
ECONOMIC INSTABILITY&MENANCES	14-20
WHAT IS EDUCATION	21-30
KINDS OF EDUCATION	31-43
EFFECTS OF ECONOMIC INSTABILITY	44-125
EFFECTS OF EDUCATION	126-243
INHIBITING VALUES TO EDUCATION	244-271
CONCLUSION	272-283
OUR CONTACTS	284

ISBN-978-978-961-195-9

ACKNOWLEDGMENT

I quite appreciate all who are always with me, that show their concern imminently and constantly to my living and concern to my making.

Though, the long list might not be incorporated in the book, but as a matter of fact, names must be mentioned because, these are the gods that God had created me through their warmth counsel and fathomless love. They are essential because, even when I go astray, they are never departed or think of not being with me, but keep on showing me a redirection on the better path to be made with tender affection.

My dearest wife, Tope and my Children, Tomiwa & Adedamola, I salute your courage to accept me and my destiny.

My biological parent, and the adopted parents with unlimited nature of parental tender care; The Very Rev.&Late Mrs J.A.Adeniji (RTD), Sir&Rev.Mrs A.B.A. Aladekomo, Daddy & Late Mummy Ayo Oni, Daddy&Mummy Dipo Komolafe, The Very Rev.&Mrs Ayo Richards, Mr&Mrs Amos Adeniran, The Very Rev.&Mrs Olatunde Onadipe,Daddy Engr&Mrs.Lana Odutola, Sir&Rev Mrs Robert Odaize. Without God making you a helper of my destiny, I would not have been able to have what it takes to have the structure in place.

To my siblings,Bro Dapo,Segun,Wemimo,Oyinade,Florence,

you are very precious to my making and dearest to me.

My friends that are always there for me, Yemo Adegbite, Dipo Sobande, e.t.c. I quite appreciate you.

So also, my friend & personal assistant, Wale Adeshina, you are cherished.

And lastly, those who have touched my life in absolute immensurable manner, Dr.O.Odubanjo, Princess Aderemi Adebowale, Bro Akin Leoso, Bro Ola Oyinloye, e.t.c. I quite appreciate your effort and faithfulness towards my making.

Methodist Church Nigeria and the Spiritual Fathers, Wesley Chapel, Lekki, City Mission Methodist Church and hosts of the other Churches, thank you for your Spiritual support.

I pray that God in His infinite mercy will keep you and bless you in His abundance blessing to flourish and be mightily blessed in all your endeavours. Thank you and God bless.

Tope Adeniji

Top Method Ventures Enterprises,

Lagos, Nigeria.

West Africa.

+234-803-718-4404 OR +234-808-093-5806

ECONOMIC MENANCES AND INTRINSIC VALUES OF FORMAL AND INFORMAL EDUCATION AS REMEDY.

INTRODUCTION

Education is light and power to the enviable world. Education has the capability to translate the most imperfect economy to the economy of great value that attracts tourist and all other function from her neighboring countries. There is no doubt that an economy that lives without adequate education creates her doom by herself. Going by the series of the experiences in most of the West Africa countries, one can deduce that the nature of the education given were very questionable compares with the nature of the existing education in the advance world. Education is programmed in such a way to have a meaningful impact in the society of their drilling and acquisition other than being based on the theoretical standard. The nature of the education in existence in the economy determines the outcome of the performances of the economy. Education carries major weight on the discovery of the necessary contents and values that can be simply applied to generate the expectation in the economy.

However, a worthwhile education should be a necessity not a choice for an economy that is looking at the growth and development in the present and nearest future. Though it sounds very interesting and easy but very ambiguous to have it fulfilled if the adequate provision is not made. But a country of an inestimable plan and futuristic intention must make it her priority.

The book is however deliberating on the vital avenue to the connection and to speedily adapt to the situation at hand. Education connects mind with the necessary views that can act as a catalyst to the transformation. It makes the mind and its contents to be spread accordingly to the necessary avenues that can derive the radical change in its formation. To be connected, there is no doubt to having an appropriate education that can necessitate its importance.

Education as an avenue to expand in the scope of thinking is a very excruciating issue that the book will look into. What this means is that, the kind of the education that one exposes to matters on the kind of view and projection he makes. Something must be seen in the context of the realm higher or beyond what an eye can see before they can be materialized. And to be frank, a qualitative education and demonstrable education is the channel towards seeing beyond ordinary.

One may consider orientation and injection of value as a very special outcome of a good education. Education is an act of orientating, passing across of the information from a source to the end point, making clarification on a subject matter, teaching on information that one is not acquitted with to make the relevant values. There might not be injection of value in the society without receiving the standard orientation or passing through a training session or a due education.

Therefore, orientation and injection of value are subject to the consideration of the thought of the book.

The actual stage at which the world is, in term of technology, innovation and her preparedness to step ahead in her various dimension can not but be traced to the impact made so far in line with the education being exposed to.

The book will look into the aspect of defining the meaning of education, kinds of education which are well known to every one, effects of education on the economy, inhibiting values of education, and conclusion.

We have numerous consideration and point that the book will leverage on as we go into the discussion of the expectation of the formal and informal education on the economy instability and recession.

ECONOMY INSTABILITY/MENANCES

Economy instability can be said to be a time of pain and agony or having a fluctuation that are not friendly with the citizenry. It is a state at which the salary that the employee receives is not enough to take care of his wellbeing. Excess money is often used for the purchase of the small commodity, and the small commodity that the excess cash can pick up might be fake and unauthentic. The prices of the commodity are massively affected, the sellers complain on the cost of their commodity while the buyers also complain at the point of buying the commodity for the onward consumption. At the cause of economic instability and recession, the products that are not essential are often left for the ones that are very compulsory which automatically set many of the witty industry liquidated.

Economic instability might be said to be the time of hardship or recession. It is a stage at which the available money in the circulation are redundant in the bank account for the reason of the uncertainty in the investment of the organizations or committing them to the activities that can yield back their profit. This stage often drift the attention of the populace away from what they can contribute to the developmental aspect of the economy, but rather, they tend to foresee the hazard of the incumbent situation and the negative aspect of its contribution to the economy.

What constitute economy instability are often those things that if they have been implemented at the very time of need would have prevented such hardship. A proper orientation and drilling towards a very productive end means can not be over emphazised at the stage of having a preventive measure to the economic instability. It is a thing of structure, which means that, if there is foundational problem, it will surely be revealed in the nearest future, which might turn to a very long stand stillness and inadjustment.

The corrective measures of the economic instability are very much available, but the correctiveness is in association with digging deep into the root which could have been covered for years. The very best preventive measure is however to have a standard working toward the projected plan for the future of the economy, and electing the adequate and functional leaders that are technocratically responsible for the execution of the projected vision.

Sometimes, when it occurs, it can be easily managed or controlled, but not often. The major problem at hand is never what the mind should pounder on at the time of regulating or adusting the economic instability, but to be able to look into the smaller activities that can necessitate the indigenous pillars to the solution of the matter.

Many at times, the leaders are passionate on exterminating the prevailling constitute of side effect of the economic instability, but they are failing on the manipulation and twisting of the policy to work in line with the adjustment. Life is a practical place, the issues in her must be handled in a practical manner, and the issues that are enveloped in life are resolvable in a radical circumstance. So also, the application of the necessary adjusment must be made suitable for the purpose of having a genuine change therein.

Teacher might not be needed to measure the present situation or effect of the economic instability before it is revealed to the whole populace. Every other things might be kept away from the people living in an economy, but the operation in the economy will never hide its impact on the condition of the general citizenry. However, the reaction of the people can not be attributable to the opponent party or the set of the individuals that are willing to sabotage the effort of the government, but the true nature of the impact of the governance on the economy.

Economic instability should be a time at which all hands are meant to be on the deck, but it is mostly its reversal in the developing world. Sincerely, immediately there is a gap while struggling to have solution, it brings about conflictory motive to handle the situation, and to have a remedy. There might not be any transformation without having the due consideration of the state of mind that can work in a peaceful way to prevail over the issue. Therefore, to create a lasting solution to the difficulties that might be introduced by the economic instability, there must be rationale to straight thinking, strange action and the ability to articulate its effectiveness.

Lucky enough, virtually all the economy that are witnessing the side effect of the economic instability are loaded with the varieties of resources and the components that can quickly act as the catalyst to the end and termination of the consequence of the economic depression and instability. The tactic to put an end to the problems should however be made indigenous mechnics and tactics in other to have a lasting solution.

CHAPTER ONE

WHAT IS EDUCATION?

It is an act of injecting value and knowledge that can produce result in term of development and advancement to the old nature or current nature of the situation in one's immediate environment and the world at large. The above interpretation is looking at the education as an act or practice that comes with result. It is looking at the education to be an avenue to convert ideology to value and tool to make a decision that can stand as an agent to the forwardness and advancement. The illustration looks at the education as a knowledge that makes provision for resultful production and visible positive consequences for the developmental and advancement on both the old and new nature of situation. And it has to do with the actual place of its experimentation, which must be its immediate environment or the world in holistic. The definition stipulated that without education, there might be a minute or no positive change in the global world.

This can be said to be a process of being furnished with the adequate information that can create or re create a man or an avenue to be gainfully processed or nurtured to know the instances of need, the solution and how to apply the solution while the economic benefit is optimumly put into consideration often a time. On the other hand, this definition is talking on the input of information into the system of the human being or any other agents that are made to constitute change and transformation. Also, it is addressing the need of the information or converted value to create a certain thing or the other. This simply implies that, the information and values are for purposes of creation and creating specific purpose towards a course or an intention. However, it is an avenue to be well nurtured and processed to be able to identify what are the needs and lack in the society or area at which human being lives. Not only that, but to give attention to the provision of the solution and its application for the economic benefit and consideration.

It is an act of formatting the mind to be well upgraded to attend to the issues, consequences and solution. This definition is similar to the one we have enumerated before now, but the slight difference is the aspect of having formatted mind. When mind is formatted, it means that, the old nature of the thinking is wipped away for the new notion and thinking. In likelihood to formatting a system (computer), there will be total nullification or extermination of the content therein, and a reload after the formatting. This often comes with new information, but most of the old information stored in other gadget that are relevant can be re-installed. When mind is upgraded, it can access the immediate issues, the consequences of the issues and proffer the necessary solution accordingly. The definition is only saying that, education assists to know that we live with the issues of all sorts around us, and that the issues can be positive or negative in nature, while a substantial solution is given due to the quality of the education received.

It is an act of learning and passing through the path that introduces world to humanity. This is saying that, education is a phase of moving through the learning process that introduces the world as it is and her requirements, and what the world expect from you and I. ordinarily, if a man is born in isolation, he will surely live a life. But the nature of the life might be so crude and inexposed other than having the privilege to access information, which means he has structure to develop his own ideology. The definition looked into the importance of the structure and introduction of life to the new born baby to know the various concept and provision to have an excelling ending.

It is a state of transforming emptiness to fulfillment and success. The definition is looking at the emptiness of purpose, of mind and of the nature of the world at the point of birth. The emptiness are interchanged through the process of learning different things that can be part of languages, culture, formal education, informal education, behavioral pattern, moral, e.t.c . The definition however concluded that, all these structures, information and values should be subjected to success. Education hence means the state of creating resourceful elements to the fulfillment of the planned success or foresight.

It has to do with the intention of making no record for impossibility and creating the mind of having a deep thought that can lead to expansion. The definition is looking at the ability to think ahead or above the impossibility of all sorts, to have the mind set that there is solution to all issues around you and I. When one can see the possibility of all sorts around him, there is every tendency of the deep thought on what should be a way ahead or remedy to the prevailing issues. Thinking above the impossibility is an act of having a resounding deep thought to have a relative expansion in one's logic to accomplish.

It has to do with the intention that leads to a standard of living and taking care of the associated economic issues by making provisions for them as a result of its attracted benefit and taking care of them, that is, monetary policy, fiscal policy and other associated issues that are contributing to the depression and recession of the economy. It is discussing on the restructuring of the defects and adjustment of all sorts to make the economy viable and conducive for the living. The aspect of the economic benefit that makes one to be involved in the economic function (working) was not exonerated. The definition simply identified education to be an avenue to meet up with the standard that makes living meaningful and conducive.

However to study out of my personal definition by looking into the dictionary meaning of education, it is termed as the process or art of imparting knowledge, skill and judgment. It is termed as facts, skills and ideas that have been learnt or learned either formally or informally. These definitions are looking at the skills or talents, and how they disseminate value or impart other lives with what they have as content, what they can give and the way of having a judgmental decision on their result's acceptability and dis-acceptability.

In the definition we have been able to extract, it is deduced that, education is both formal and informal in nature. Ideas and innovation can come into existence as a result of attending institution or school or technical colleges and learning other handiwork, while we have those who had never been to any school being widely learned as a result of their exposure. But for the advantage of the reader and as a result of the immediate situation of most of the Africa countries, it is quite essential to attend a formal institution or school to a certain level to have the basic education that can stand as a structure for an informal education of your choice.

The definitions had made us to understand that education is the soul of an enviable economy, and an avenue to the proper growth and development.

CHAPTER TWO

KINDS OF EDUCATION

The two kind of education which are well noticed or harbors other forms of education are simply the formal and informal education.

Formal education is a Western education brought to us as African nations. It entails reading, speaking and learning in an official manner, and making provision for certification at the end of the period of time enslated for such a program. In formal kind of education, there is often syllabus or guide line that stipulates the intention of the program or the orientation. These set of program must be well treated from a stage to another till the entire topics or area of concentration is covered. Students' are often given the assignments to have researches on the complex tasks or studies to have diversified solutions provided. There are testings in the laboratory and the entire world. Formal education often has a general acceptable principle and practices which must be universal most at times.

On the other hand, the informal education has to do with the technical studies. This means that, the student might not write anything down at the point of learning. It is often on the job learning, which means that, the student learn the diversified tricks of accomplishing a task in each day of his certification or coming to work. Here, it is more tedious because you may not have anything written to reflect on after the work. All what you can acquire are instill in you on daily basis and the experiences till you are graduated. Any event or trick that is attained without being understood must be asked immediately else, there might not be any other opportunity to witness such anymore. Learning here is in each second or on each operation that takes place.

Though, in most of the Africa countries, the informal education is termed to be subjected to the formal education, but I want to quickly use this means to have a bit of corrective measure on the opinion that, both forms of education are quite pertinent at the point of having growth and development in the economy. The sincere part of it is that, the formal education that is not radical and hypothentical might be an impediment to the advancement of the nation if care is not given to nurturing the upcoming on the application of the studies of the citadel of learning.

To have an economy that is working or efficient, there is need for the technocrat to be in place. Anything that can be seen but that can not be attained is often termed to be a dream or waste in term of time resources and its reality context.

Hence, the need for cordial relationship of both formal and informal education towards the greatness of the economy and her viability; to attain the height of full exploitation and achievement.

Formal Education;

School ; this is refer to a place, environment or class room at which the students' are gathered together for the purpose of learning or receiving information.

Certificated qualification; this can be any form of education or training that is back up with certificate. This often takes place in the class room too.

Professional courses; there are different professional bodies in the world, and each of them do their professional courses. This makes whosoever that has such a certificate to be qualified for the function of the profession. What this means is that, one might not go the school and yet, he is qualified on the field of his or her professional line or body. Such qualification can be ACCA, and every other qualification within the context of the scope of the professional body.

Training centre; training centre does not necessary mean that the training is core education. It can be on the other related issues such as moral, human capital development, facilitation, motivation, way of life , e.t.c. this form of training is as well back up with certificate, and the certificates can be an added advantage to the credentials.

Technical training; there are many technical schools having various type of different handiwork in their curriculum. This is very similar to the informal technique, but a hybrid of it. There are class rooms and workshops at which whatever that are thought are experimented compares with the school training which might be theoretical in nature all through the studies.

Seminary and religious school; here, the focus of the studies is concentrated on the doctrine of the religion under consideration. There are numerous religious, and each of them has various centres at which the new clergy are introduced appropriately to the school of thought of the religion. In such schools, certificate are given to the grandaunts to show or proof that such an individual is well read and appropriate for the purpose of teaching the doctrine and interpreting the content of their spiritual books. e.t.c

Seminar, symposium and talk show; these are another set of the training that might be hidden under formal training, but they might not come with the issuance of certificate or qualification.

Informal Education;

Learning of skill; talents and traits are inbuilt and can be learnt from the possesor of the traits and talents. Take for an example, dancing, singing, running, comedy, e.t.c. they can be learnt without going to school. It only involves one's ability and willingness to have it accomplished.

Knowledge; this can be series of ways that knowledge is passed across to the world. Knowledge is power and this is the only means at which there can be increase in all levels. Tricks of doing various things can be administered or related on at the course of informal education. Though, this is not in formal language or does it entails writing of books or point on the paper. The actual way at which the knowledge is disseminated is what has made it to be either formal or informal. Mostly, in the informal set up, local dialect and languages are of use.

Learning of handiwork; handiwork in contrary is an act of making things with the craft knowledge. It is out rightly learning of the skill that can produce a practical result in line with the one's level of creativity and dexterity. This is termed to be aprenticeship. Occupation such as fashion design, farming, learning of business, shoe making, mechanic, e.t.c. are core kind of this nature.

Personal growth and development; this is an instance of learning through what someone knows. Actually, the situation around you and I are sufficient to create the desire needs of the world. Personal development is an action that takes place as a result of what one can access in him or her. It is the direct experimentation of reasoning ability in the context of what one posseses. Growing personally is however termed as informal education because it has no general acceptance of practice.

Exposure ; exposure has to do with the priviledge that one has as regards his ability to study vastly and to travel near and far. At the course of reading or travelling around, he is proned to various ideas and systematic way of learning. He can access information in the books as if he is closed to the source and at the point of relating with the different types of people, he is priviledged to be better enlightened on the standard ways of having a successful ending on different types of transactions, undertakings and endeavors.

Reading books and new paper; just as mentioned aboved, reading books, journal, magazine, news paper are very essential to the developmental value. They bring information to the arm's length of whosoever that is indulged in such an attribute and gives the opportunity to have series of information that can be developed on. A man is an embodiment of what he knows, and sincerely, one can only operate at the realm of his ability to think. The more the information are accessed, the more the logical strenghtability to convert chances to opportunity. Since ability to read can be learnt outside the school and the formal setting, this can be made to be informal when it is not proccessed in a formal structure.

Rumour and grape vine; rumors and grape vine are very essential when one is checking on their positive implication. Sometimes, what one hears turn him to be who he is meant to be, when the information that are crucial for the developmental purpose are established, they encourage such an individual with the information to have an edge way over others. Information extracted from the rumor and grape vine can be termed as education when they are imparting and educational.

The little discussion can be very essential to the analysis of the kind of the education and to differentiate and understand the reason why they are termed to be what they are made to be.

CHAPTER THREE

EFFECTS OF THE ECONOMIC INSTABILITY

There are numerous effects of the economic instability. The fact remains that even things that are meant to be working positively might be translated to their opposite nature. Economic instability makes the populace to often think of not having the due hope for the provisions that their economy can offer them. It is said to be a turn around towards the desirable expectation of the populace. It is a time of complaining and passing through the phase of difficulty that can be well noticed in the lives of the residence and her economy. It can as well be termed as the time of drought, in which what are planted requires additional effort to be fruitful. Any nation that experiences this, might find it very cumbersome to have anything meaningful to achieve because the prymary aim and the perspective of thought would be strictly directed to the avenue of having the effect of the economy instability controlled. Hence, these are the little points that can be enlisted at the point of writing this book;

1. Unemloyment- One of the most distinctive effects of the economic instability is unemloyment. At the time of economic instability, it is often very difficult to secure job. Most of the people that are working work harder to secure their work because of the inavailability of openings in the organization. It means that, if one is not creative

and understand how best to apply the academic acquisition, it might be difficult if not impossible to be involved in any economic function. Economic instability shrinks the available avenues and lower productivity, its aftermath effect is directly or indirectly on the employees. Organization or group of business that has nothing to produce or do might not need the staff to be employed.

2. Devaluation of currency- A productive nation is a nation that has the tendency to grow to her state of planning. There is vast colossal negative effect of the economic instability on the currency of any nation at which the evidence

is pronounced. When a nation has nothing to produce, he has nothing to sell and transact on. Sincerely, one of the major agents of correcting the value of currency is through the use of exportation. It is only the producing nation that can make production that can be exported to the other neighbouring countries. The higher in the exportation will determine the quantity of the other nation's currency and value that will be made in exchange for the commodity. This instance however creates the opportunity to have value that can add up to the finance of the economy for the developmental purpose. This however means that the economy will enjoy more financial strength ahead of her counterpart, which translates to revaluation of currency. Instead of this experience, at the phase of recession or instability, the value of the currency of the Nation that witness the odd in the economy deteriorated and makes the market across the world unsuitable.

3. High cost of living-By this, I mean the cost of making provision for the daily needs is high. There are several needs of human on daily basis. It depends on the selection of one or some among the insatiable wants and desire of the individuals. Human beings must eat on daily basic, must drink, put on cloths and purchase

various other commodities that make their daily living appreciable and conducive. At the expense of these desire, the cost of having the desire are very high as a result of the instability that the economy in question is facing. When there is economic instability, the value at which commodity are purchased are extremely higher compares with the state of having stable economy. This however translates to the high cost of the standard of living.

4. High cost of farm product- the farm products are always very high and expensive to buy when there is appearance of economic instability. The cost of planting and managing it is very expensive, the cost of

transportation is high and more other expenses that are incurred before the products are made available to the last consumer. The accumulation of these effects however leads to the expensive rate of the production of the farm produce.

5. Transportation is high- The cost of moving from a place to another and of conveying the products and commodity are extremely expensive as mentioned before hand. The point remains that, the transporter are part of the economy too and they must be able to adjust their dealing to the tune of meeting up with the demand of the economy. They pay their house rent, they pay

for their bills, they pay school fees, e.t.c. they try to adjust their activities to such a standard that can meet up with their desire and requirement to meet up with a standard that can enhance them good living.

6. Inflation- All what we have been studying is in connection with inflation. Inflation can be said to be a situation whereby excess of physical cash are used to pick up small quantity of commodity. It is a situation whereby the prices of the commodity are increasing in an abnormal way. It is termed to be a time at which the purchasing power is made to be totally weakened at the point of transaction. However,

inflation is one of the major constitute of the economic instability.

7. High cost of education- This chapter is to examine the effect of the economic instability in the economy on the education. Since, the entire system operates in the economy, high cost of education can not be exonerated out of the major defects. The high education drives many of the population to divert their interest to other economic functions that can generate immediate returns other than expending on the education that might eventually not be productive and lucrative to them in a short time. They are always eager to have

such jobs that can take care of their immediate needs. High cost of education has made majority of the growing ones that are intelligent having no opportunity to go to school. In some nations, the younger ones are pampered to attend institution, apart from the payment of the school fees, they still give them pocket allowances while some carter for their feeding in the school. One of the determinants of the greatnesss of any nation is the ability to avail the younger ones a qualitative education. In the absence of this, the developmental rate falls in the nearest future. The concern of both the government and the school proprietor are to make profit not because of the passion and interest they have in given out the knowledge. Hence, since the economic instability creates unnecessary panic and fear, the exorbitant amount charge discourages the parents and guardians, and the element of gridiness surfaces in the educational sector.

8. Instability in the policy- Numerous policies are made and changed during the economic instability. This is an avenue to know or adjust the economy to the nature of the system the economy is operating on. Policies are often changed and made to be suitable for the governance instead of the public most especially when the elected representative are

not tactical and dynamic in nature. Their intention is to regulate or abolish the issues in the economy, but the rightful restructuring are left untouched while policies are twisted and other avenues in their capability are made to be chief solution to the economy upgrade. Therefore, if care is not taken, there will continually be changes instead of facing out the issues or looking for the best way to give a reasonable solution. Most of the issues that lead to the economic instability are human inactiveness. They are mostly generated by the action that are meant to be acted on but never did, or did haphazardly. Ordinarily, when the system are not working systematically or in line with the provision of the plans and structure in place, it often leads to economic issues which might be handled by those who do not know the beginning of such problem and do not have what it takes to study them to have a lasting solution to them, to have a more difficult outcome on the prevailing issues. In the struggle or initiation to have an adjustment, however, most of the representatives or leaders at the point of making adjustment are leading the economy into a more deteriorated and degenerated condition. As a result of trial and error, they manipulate the policies from time to time to be suitable for the purpose of the governance instead of having a solution to the crisis. As the struggle continues at the aspect of having adjustment to the issues, policies are changed from time to time. The aspect of the periodical changes in the policies of the government mostly when the ideas are not presence to resolve the issues is very imortatnt to be cross examined at the point of relating on the economic instability.

9. High cost of importation and exportation- The cost of importation is extremely high in the sense that, it takes a very huge amount to pay for the commodity and convey the products to the country. The balance of payment is extremely impaired and affected negatively. Also, at the point of exportation, large amount of money are set aside

to carry out such activities. The nature of the valuation of the currency is quite very essential at the point of cross examining the cost the exportation and importation. Therefore, without argument, the effect of the economic instability must be vivid on the exportation and importation in an economy.

10. Brain drift- When there is no form of encouragement for the younger ones, most especially the ones with the creative knowledge and talents, they prefer to move out of the economy to another economy where their talent and creativity can be appluaded and encouraged. It is so painful to know how to do

something, and yet, you are relegated or made to be as if you do not know anything. Knowledgeable individuals are very sensitive to the issue of being counted as non entity and trying to adjust to the abnormality. Many are the great produced and born mighty men and women that had left their respective economy as a result of their inability to make a reasonable impact. They had given their very best in one way or the other, but yet, their impact is not productive. They however prefer to be where they can be well appreciated and have a meaningful contribution. The most pathetic aspect of it is that, not until most of these ones are celebrated in the other world or economy, they are never reckoned with in their contries or economy. The issues of brain drift can not be over emphazised at the point of looking into the economic instability and recession.

11. Desire and urge for money- At the time of economic instability, the urge and the desire for money is quite higher. The populace runs after the wealth or riches without minding how they are found or attained. The creativity and self initiative are often converted to fraudulent foresight and things that can make or create money without any stress or any meaningful economic function undertaking. Economic instability that is not

controlled is detterent to the economic, and can cause a colossal destruction. The youth are unwilling to do or perform any work any more, while the younger ones that are working most especially at the sensitive places are turned to greedy beings and often engage in fraudulent activities.

12. Undue panic and speculation- When things are not working out fine, people often engaged in all forms of rumour that are liable for the undue panic and speculation that even add up more of the pain to the situation at hand. Economic instability brings up panic and speculation unnecessarily to the world of the citizenry and system of the

governance and this often aggravate the issues when the government can not immediately find a solution to the problems. There is always tension, panic and speculation that make people to get too greedy about the material things. Most of the available commodities are hoarded for the sake of selling them at a higher cost. Physical cash that should be invested into the industrialization are invested in personal porfolio and investments, many even have cash buried under the soil, some are in the possession of the exorbitant values of vehicles that are not useful to them. There is always a preparation for the time that has not come or for the instances that might not emanate in the nearest future.

13. Greediness and embezzlement- Quite annoying and disturbing that the set of the highest paid allowances and salary earner are often indulged in the act of embezzlement and fraud. Where there is no provision for the future of the generation by the government, they tend to be greedy whenever they are given the priviledge or availed the opportunity. No matter the worth of what has been stolen, the mind set of not yet comfortable with the amount stolen comes up in their mind. We have experienced many citizen with vast money buried

under the soil or ground. Many do not even know how many account they have or where they have the accounts as a result of too many greed or urge for material things. Economic instability constitutes panic, and create greediness, and not only that, it leads to the embezzlement of fund at any giving time to act as representative of the others. I have thousands of friends that had told me a lot of things because of the present predicament, that, they will steal if they are fortunate to be leader. Some are already serving in one capacity or the other as representative now, what is the justification of them not stealing now? Also, I have done many survey on the people, the major outcome is that, when you get there you must just quickly pack up yours before you are either flushed out or led out. The point is that, the economic instability is the chief cause of this attribute and the mind set when one looks critically and in-depthly into their constitute.

14. Poor facility in the local hospital- if you are very healthy and hail, it worths to be grateful to God. Try to look around into the hospitals, mostly in the developing countries, you will definitely be downcasted and embarrassed with the facility provided and their operations. Most of the facilities are out dated and crude. No wonder, it is a habitual

standard for many of those ones that have stolen huge amount of money or that are of better opportuned to travel from time to time to either examine their health or for treatment outside the country. The funds that are meant to be the source of improvement and upgrade have been embezzled or stolen for private use. Self centredness is one of the major issues that erupt in the instance of economic instability. The government must however take a full flesh action to seeing that economy is well checked and balanced to avoid the instability that has been the deterent to the growth and development from the time immemorial.

15. Poor infrastructure and amenities- Just like the scenario just mentioned as regards the hospital development and issues. There are thousands of things that have been approved in the time past, and their money has been paid for accordingly, but yet, they are not visible or executed. However, the set of individuals that are meant to be regulator to these hideous acts are being buried with extortion and blind folded with the extention of the poisonous cake given to them. Most of the countries are found acting seasonal films with various episodes. When there is failure on the part of the governance to do what they are supposed to do, but not attained. The citizenry find excuses to

misbehave. The total money that is meant to be available for the use of the funding amenities and infrastructure are shared among the minority for their personal use. The populace complains and yet, the set of the individuals that are responsible for the cause of the degeneration as well complain. In nut shell, the logic behind the inadequacy performances is in connection with the prevailing instability in the economy.

16. Coverage of the good ideas and thought. There is no one that can not think, there is no one without a skill or the other, but before a man can have an accurate thinking, he must have a stable mind and an

environment that is so conducive for such purpose. Environment of study is quite very essential at the point of having a qualitative and standard lecture and information assessed across to the student's. So also, to have a good thought and reasoning, there must be a conducive environment. An economy that is operating under a tensed situation may not really have anything to offer. The people living within the geographical zone are often very far away from the ability to think on the realistic issues that can lead the nation ahead. A good economic structure is quite essential to have the best outcome and the best resourceful information that can lead the nation under discussion ahead. The possibility and the urge to attain goal is essential to the degree at which an economy can operate. In the situation of economic instability, the urge is reduced and the thinking of the possibility is no where to be found. Ideas are buried and thoughts are forgone when they could not see the encounraging elements and factors that should be a boost to their contribution.

17. Poor industrialization- The investors believe in the return on their investment and their profitability. All investors or organization owners are of the interest in how best they can generate their revenue or income to have a better

opportunity. The nature of the opportunity that most of the organizations are exposed is directly or indirectly connected with the nature of the economy in which they are found. However, to appeal to the populace or lure them into industrialization, there must be factors that must stand as encourager and which they must see operating. Industrialization is avenue at which the best of the nation in term of creating values and converting raw materials can be proven to the other world or continent. It is an avenue of coming into the organization or creating an industry for the sake of the use of the creativity and innovation within the nation. Industrialization has to do with the improvement in the gross domestic products of a nation. This is the total amount of the products produced in the economy at a time of consideration. The higher the number of produce or quantity of produce definitely leads to the competitive economy that can be in existence. Industrialization is the major or core strength of nation building, and when a critical look is given to the economies that are found wanted in one way or the other, one will definitely discover that, their aspect of industrialization is nothing to write about. A nation must have something she produces, and such a product must be available for the exportation, which automatically affect the balance of payment of such a nation. So, practically, a bad economic issue affects the efficiency of the industrialization negatively and discourages the investors to have the mind or intention to have industrialization in place.

18. Liquidation of industry and organization- Unlike the point mentioned ahead. That was contemplating on the industrialization. On this particular point, the effect of the economy is seen in its hazardous way of killing or exterminating the existing industries and organization. When the industry or organization is made available in the environment that is not friendly to them, they are

exposed to limited time frame to collapse. Many are the well named industries that are no more as a result of the harsh economy on them. So, the point I am driving at is that, the nature of the economy is responsible for the life span of the industry or organization. When an economy is established on the fertile land or structure, there is every tendency of having a full fleshed and greater opportunity that can lead such an organization or industry ahead. Therefore, the issue of economic stability is not, but a compulsory to be rectified to have increase and the fulfillment of the production and servicing sector of the economy.

19. Lack of link between the production and servicing organization- Services and the production sector of the economy are meant to have an interrelated association in the economy. In the case of having one out of the two not functional leads to the gap of the consideration. There is no way servicing industries can add up to the economy without the need of the productive sector of the economy. The type of the relationship that exists is so closed to the level of transferring resources from one to another. What I am saying is this, at the point at which a servicing organization has made its profit, it must find it very compulsory to affect the lives of the productive industries with a certain

percentage of whatever made or gained. This leads to expansion and increasement in the industrialization and connotes an additional gain to the servicing organizations. So also, the presence of the industrialization on its production of various commodities is very useful for the use of the servicing organization. At a state at which the industry is made incapacitated and only few industry are present denotes that, there will definitely be an urge for the importation of common raw materials and resources that can be locally produced which might not favor the organizations in the context of the economy in discourse. What I am saying is this, there must be a cordial relationship between the servicing and industrial organization, and the absence of good economic stability might be a hindrance to a qualitative nature of relationship that should exist between the two parties.

20. Loan is discouraged- In line with what I have been examining, when there is no assurance of having a breakthrough or edge way on the investments, the good investors do not risk it. Loan that are meant to be borrowed for the purpose of establishing or creating various kind of innovation are left in the financial houses. People prefer to make use of their resources to create what can fetch them and their family their daily living than going extra mile to

borrow. A stable economy aids increase in borrowing strength and willingness to make a valuable impact in the economy while the reverse is discouragement to loan.

21. Hard working is discouraged- People tend to move to the economy that is suitable and friendly with the compensation of their hard working. The insentive to the hard working is very relevant to the encouragement of the people to work harder, and for every other indolent people around to cultivate the habit of giving their best for the purpose of the economic activities. Many of the advance countries are over populated because of the typical reason of having an adequate

compensation for both the work and hard working. In some of these countries, the over time is even made available for those who are strong to go beyond their respective duration or time. The logic I am trying to potray is that, economic instability is prone to having the populace lazy and indolent. Instead of being aggressive to the hard working, people tend to look for an alternative route of making easy money when they are not treated well accordingly to their input. This is as a result of the suppression of the encouragement on the task undertaken, and payment of commensurable competitive compensation to the workers. As a result of this, minds are translated from its productive status to struggling and finding an avenue to acquire wealth under must. Before having a proper hard working minded individuals, there must be provision for an insentive that is worth while compares with the input, and the set of the people that are very active and industrious must have something to show as reference for it.

22. The desire for formal and informal education is lowered- Education is quite very relevant to the greatness of the nations. Any nation without adequate information is a nation that is planting her extermination by herself in both present and in the nearest future. Education comes in

both formal and informal ways, and they are the avenue at which minds are opened to the things that are not known, things that might take time to be known and the things that are well proven and tested in life. No knowledge is wasted, it depend on the actual perspective of receiving the information. Information not relevant to one might be the most expensive information to another, while that of the other might be the best information that can cause translation in one's life. Information comes up around you and me every day, but only the smart thinkining men are often congnizance of them. There should be the urge and passion for education, most especially by the younger generation. This makes a very fundamental and impressive architectural pattern of the expected world or economy of the generation focus. Information must be made available constantly for the growth of the people in the nation, and this however translate to the effective performance of the economy under discussion. Before a perfect education can however be in place, there must be economy stability that can encourage the mind and the willingness of the men to move along with their desire. In the point raised before hand, I was trying to say that the mind of the people are focused on how to generate their daily need other than becoming hard working, so also, in this very point I am trying to analyze, the exorbitant price and school fees is an impediment on the part of those who are willing to further or go to school. More so, there are many individuals that might not be willing to demonstrate their value or learn a work or the other as a result of the instability. For one to have a distinctive desire or urge for both formal and informal education, there must be an economy that creates a conducive environment for it.

23. Cost of production is high- All organization of all kinds is into the business of profit making. Whatever that is purchased for the intention

of the production must be taken into the consideration at the point of fixing price. At least there is need to have profit on any production to be able to pay for wages, production, bills, rates and other necessity during the production processings. When the price of the raw materials is high, this automatically translates to the increase in the cost of the product eventually. To experience continuity in business, industry or organization must be able to get to the equilibrium level if at all it is not making large profit. And sincerely, when there is devaluation of currency, industry buy raw material at a higher cost both within and overseas. This often makes the cost of their products or service to be very unreasonable, and makes the standard of living to be very expensive. The devilment in the high cost of the production can directly be attributed to the state of the economy. When economy is glowing, the effect or result must definitely be felt on the organization she encompasses.

24. Lost of interest in the governance- The populace is meant to have the confidence in the governance of the people they elected into the power or their leaders. The moment the interest is lost in the authority begins the very great problem and challenges that such a government might be exposed to. The

government is in structure for the management of the resources to the optimum level of making life very interesting to the citizenries. But in case of having the opposite of the result being executed, the confidence and security is replaced with biasness, criticism and looking ahead for the change of power. Lost of interest in the governance might cause the populace never to have anything meaningful to be contributed to the society or the economy. When the citizenries develop the interest in the governance, they have enormous contribution they offer to the government that can upgrade their conscent and concept to meet with the need of the economy. The people in any economy often know their needs and how the need can be given solution to, but they might have little or no capability to act accordingly on having the solution. However, at the point at which the government and the populace are in cordial relationship, poeple show their interest in the governance by making them to know what they want and the possibility of having them sorted. When poeple are not comfortable, they have little or no interest or concern in whatever the government does. So, economic instability can be an avenue to have a lost of interest or desire for the governance.

25. Change of power or governance- People are not too keen about the change of power mostly when the economy is handled by the elected authority or representatives to the best state. Though, there are exceptional cases at which there must be change of power as a result of exceeding the term that is slated for such a government. Many representatives have been in power for more than 20 to 30 years, in this nature of situation, it is most likely people agitate for change. But when it is otherwise, and things are not moving as expected, poeple clamour for change of the leaders or vote them out in the next immediate election or revollt. What I am saying is that, when the government falls

below the average level of performance, citizenry might conclude to have a transformation for the betterment of their lives. This can however be seen in their action and agitation to demonstrate their interest in the change of the governance or to vote them out when due. A good economy can elongate the term of the authority in charge, whereas, when there is instability, it might not make them to stay for a very long period of time, but having their tenure being witness with uproar and society unrest.

26. Transfer of aggression- sometimes, one might ask a simple question that what can be wrong with the

people around who easily get provoked and act abnormally as a result of little or no fault from anyone. The environment at which one resides or leaves has a major impact on the behavioural pattern of the individuals. There is a particular language in my economy now that says "igboro o re ri" which simly means that the environment is not laughing. Meaning that things are not in their best shape, economy is harsh on the citizens. In a situation of this nature, the type of relationship that should exist among the citizenry might not be cordial and of the standard which one should access at the point of evaluation. When things are not in good shape, people might not be able to fight with the invisible nature of life and the economy, but rather, to transfer the venger or annoyance on the individuals around them. Things that prompt issues are very insignificant when one cross examine it. What should be resolved amicably are translated to issues that are serious in nature which might be made to be a major issues. The instability in the economy is one of the major constitutes of the rancor and disarray that exist in the economy, and this often affect the repositioning and restructuring of the economy.

27. Foreign investors are discouraged- The nature of the economy has the

greatest value on the investment of the foreigners. Before any of the foreigners can attempt to come in for investment or organizing businesses, they must go through the history of such an economy of their choices. Resultful economy is considered far better than the economy that might constitute lost to the investments. When an economy is bad, it has its effect on the viability of the businesses in it, and this is the first yard stick to either attract or discourage foreign investors. In most of the African economy, many industries and organization have wounded up as a result of the nature of the economy in existence. What this implies is that, if the economy system in operation has been working out fantastically, these organizations might still be able to manage themselves. The issue of economy potency can bring the best result in term of organizational growth and industrial development. Therefore, to have the best investors or to be enrichly developed as a nation, there is need for an environment that can accommodate the growing of the business in consideration.

28. Immigrants and foreigner are discouraged- The reason why many of the other country's citizens are moving out of their respective country is because of the better environment at which they might find themselves when they have a

change of location. If the economy is perfect and accommodating, there is no need of running hecter skecter or up and down. One might be interested in paying visit to the other countries or going for excursion, but will never prefer staying out of his country to staying within. The rate at which many countries are deserted is quite alarming. I can courageously say that, if most of the citizenry of any of the African countries are given the free right of order to be migrated to USA, only few will be left. Economy that is friendly is an economy that attracts foreigners. Most of the foreigners only have the delight in the environment that is with adequate security, political stability, economy stability, employment, developmental, e.t.c .

29. Cheap sources of riches- What this means is that, people will always look out for the easy way of attaining their riches. It is quite better to have a functional economy functioning to create wealth than having a short cut to riches or making wealth. When the poeple are not sure of tomorrow, they look around for the very best way to make the money for the purpose of storing them for the time to come. Economic instability makes men to think that without having in excess, you might not be able to have tomorrow. It discourages hard working and instead, makes the

people to look out for an avenue to defraud others or to find a means of cheating at all cost. When there are too much of free fund that are not functional or funds that are generated illicitly without having any meaningful contribution on the economy, it becomes a hazard to such an economy. And the real source of having a cheap source of riches is a bad economy. Courageously, I can affirm it to you that, if the economy is at its best state, most of the leaders and the followers will never be too conscious of money or material things.

30. Poor and fake production- I mentioned some notes on the high

cost of production. Its effect and consequences on the cost of the commodity. High cost of commodity can be a hindrance to the consumption of such commodity. It can create a gap that will lead to the liquidation of the organization or industry if it has no competitive mechanism and resources. There is no organization or industry that is not of the motive to make profit, so, they give the very best of various tactic and ideas to making sure that their profit is ascertained. However, when the cost of the commodities or resources is high, the quantity to be sold are reduced and this can thereafter tell on the cost of production which might lead to the liquidation of such organization if care is not taken. Most of the organization however sees production of substandard commodities as their edge way in term of the difficulties they are confronted with. Exportation of fake material and fake products are made to have a defected production. The zeal to make money or profit at all cost over shadows the need to produce the best commodity for the consumption of the citizenry. This however is one of the hazards in relationship with the issues of the instability and recession in an economy.

31. Complaining and murmuring – I discussed about the issue of transfer of aggression in one of the topics

treated. This is another consequence which must be experienced before having transfer of aggression sometimes. When things are not going the very way at which they are growing or going, many individuals complain, many murmur. Instead of being at a state of joyful and rejoicing, one might be in a state of unhappiness and of no hope. What I am saying is that, many are at the cross junction, they do not know what to do or who to be held responsible. As a result of this, they only complain and murmur to show that they are not comfortable. They often fight themselves internally instead of fighting the cause of such abnormality.

32. Smuggling and other attrocities- When the situation of an economy gets to the level of survival of the fittest, it makes people to think of various attrocities to be involved in. One of the attrocities which is rampant is smuggling. Smuggling is an act of taking goods and commodity in and out of an economy without due approval or payment of the duties and other necessary dues. Smuggling is quite high at the period of economy recession or instability compares with when things are in good other. Smuggling can not be left out of the one of the depressive elements of the economic instability.

33. Irregular payment of salary- Economic depression and recession are examplified for irregular payment of salary and wages to the staff of the government parastatal or agencies. When there is no source of revenue or solid fountain of having income or receiving intake, and there are surplus of employee waiting or receiving salary, and quite a number of the individuals relying on the assistance of the government, the result is short of finance to take good care of the government projects. When the government are failing on their part to invest into the industrial sector that can be a source of finance, or having the ability to look around them for the resources that can be

an advantage ahead of the others, it might be difficult for such state to triump or succed. The governance must be very active and willing to be involved in the economic activities that can be a source of various opportunities for the people. At the point of the creation of the opportunity, the human capital is to be used while they receive their salary and wages accordingly from their economic contribution. Their contribution however has a certain product that comes thereafter which can be used by the people collectively, sold to the neighbouring states and at the same time be exported. When there is no activity in a state, there might be a degeneration and waste of human capital, e.t.c. that might be responsible for the incompetency to have a regular payment of the salary and wages. When money fails to create money or opportunity, it creates gap for the problems and issues that should have been taken care of or resolved.

34. Reduction in salary and wages- The issue of cut off in the salary and wages payment is quite different from the irregularity of payment of salary. In the former, salary and wages are held for months, years and the entire salary might not be paid eventually. Whereas, in this particular issue at hand, the salary and wages are cut off. For example, someone earns 70,000.00 but as a

result of economic instability has 40,000.00 to be received monthly. The most painful part of it is that, the same person will be operating on his position but the salary is reduced. The whole lots of the information associated to the irregularity in the payment of the salary are responsible for its reduction. And whenever there are any elements of this in any state, it depicts that the state or economy is not competent to handle the issue around it. Luckily enough, there is no state without the resources that can be made to create them or make a world of their own, but when the hands and mind in power can not either see or act on converting them to possibilities, they become a waste, unproductive, abadorned and negation.

35. It prevents other long time plan to be achieved- Take for an example, when someone has a head ache and has the mind to invest in a stock exchange. If the amount he has in mind is 30,000.00 to be invested, but the result of the hospital test reveals that, he needs 45,000.00 to have a proper treatment. I can tell you vividly that, if the condition is tensed, he might not even know when he will borrow more to be added up to what is at hand. To be sincere, had it been that precaution has be taken at the very initial stage of the headache, very possibly such a fellow would have only spent little

amount of money, but because of his way of handling it with levity, it becomes a serious issue. My analyses are that when what someone is meant to do is left unattended to, they become more deteriorated and complicated. So also is the issue of economic instability. When what are meant to be attained at their initial stages are failed to be accomplished, they stand to be the hindrances that are far more complicated. At the point of looking round for the remedy of the issues after they have gone beyond measure, other major assignments that are meant to be attended to are left untouched. So, when there is issue in the economy, the chief concern of the government is to have a solution to the problems, but forgetting other sectors that are meant to be touched and the future plan as a result of the pressure around their motives.

36. White collar job are celebrated- At the point of having discussion on the industrialization and coming forth with the organization, I mentioned that, when there is hardship in the economy, it affects the productivity of the industry or organization. Many industries and organizations have liquidated, many are struggling to survive and many are on recession just because of the issues of the economy. A viable economy is responsible for a better outcome of

industries and organization. This however change the mind set of many that has the motive of being creative and productive in nature. Many people are well grounded on converting one resource or the other to a finished product, but the economy in which they operate stands as mitigation to the demonstration of their skill and talents. Instead of investing or wasting time on the uncertainty, many consider travelling out, while majority opt for working in a well established organization that can withstand the pressure of the economy instability and at the same time provide for their daily needs. Though many are not comfortable with their package or monthly payment as it might never be able to take them home, but they have no option as a result of looking at it that, half bread is better than none. With this fact, many are engaged in the white collar jobs without making any effort to give a trial to be an owner of a business or initiator of an idea or a risk taker.

37. Exploitation- One of the constitute of the economic instability is exploitation. As soon as most of the owner of the existing business discovered that the employee have no option, they tend to defraud them of various condition of services and benefits such as increases in salary, health bonus, leave bonus, maternity bonus, 13th

month salary, car allowance, e.t.c. exploitation is when labour contribution to the growth and development of an organization is undermined in term of the service condition. It can be termed to be a situation whereby the compensation is not commensurate with the effort inputted. It is an avenue of using people to achieve a certain goal and objective without their maximum care. Some organization still run contract staff today just for the sake of exploitation. What I am saying is that, when there are alternatives or good economy, such act can be maximumly controlled because, there will be surpplus of varieties of jobs and work, and option that one can pick up alternatively. In the time of economy instability, one of the major issues that run around the state or economy is exploitation, and it is apparent in most of the organizations.

38. Massive retrenchment and disengagement- There is always massive disengagement and retrenchment when there is critical issues in the economy. When the Profitability margin is massively reduced, the organization and industries look out for the avenue to reduce their cost in all ramifications, and by so doing, look into the aspect of reducing the work force. Many organizations have reduced their staff tremendiously and many are still planning to do that just because

of their incapability to meet up with their expectation. It is quite very better to discontinue with the association that exist between the employer and employee than allowing them to work without being paid for the jobs they undertake. The situation of economic instability that has to do with the decrease in the productivity and sinking of the organization and industry are always very essential when mass retrenchment of the workers is examined.

39. Balance of payment is negatively affected- before there can be perfect balance of payment or having a gain over the other

economy or countries in the aspect of balance of payment, there must be massive production and convertion of resources to final products. A nation that does not engage in the massive production of commodity that can be used within and exported might not be referred to a nation that is potent enough to have a competitive balance of payment. Something must be exchanged for one another, such is a commodity for another currency or a service for the payment of the foreign currency. The transaction that transpires between a country and the other countries however are responsible for the standard or improper balance of payment. This means that, such a country receive in returns, the currency of the other countries which serve as a boost towards the availability of financial strength and economic issues. Authetically, many countries and economy could not meet up with the desire of her residents not to mention of being involved in the exportation of the commodities and services they can offer.

40. Late marriages and divorce- Sincerely, when things are moving on in a perfect order, the issue of responsibility is meant to be shared by both the husband and wife, but in case of having a tensed situation, the wife should know that the responsibilty of the husband is to take care of the children and herelf

but can stand within the gap till the situation is calm down. There are many wives that are much more sufficient than their husband in term of finance, though the amount they receive is enomous to take care of them and the family, but yet, they believe that, it is the responsibility of the husband to take care of the responsibilities even at the point of him having nothing. My argument is not in support of the husband not taking charge of their responsibility, but I am only saying that, when economy is suitable, there will be a lots of opportunities that will definitely make the husband to be engaged, and not that all alone, the salary of the wife will be buoyant enough to take care of the wife and even to be saved. Also, in the second phase of the issue on late marriage, many men are riped and old enough to have their respective wives at home, but the immediate prevailing issues around them might never allowed them to be a husband to a wife. Sometimes, most of the uncles without wives are referred to as impotent or probably that they are trying to become a "FATHER". Mostly, reverse is the case in the sense that, many are only trying to be guided and controlled not to have unnecessary responsibility. Therefore, to round it up, the issue of economy is very relevant at the point of loking into the causes of the late marriages and issue of divorce.

41. Birthrate control- There is no one without a responsibility or the other that are meant to be attended to at a time or the other. So also, when there is an agreement that leads to wedding or marriage. The fruit of the marriage is called children, and these children are under-must must be taken care of when they are given birth. Sincerely, having a wife is a huge responsibility not to mention the children. The more the number of the children you have might determine the level of your responsibility on taking care of them. However, at the point of family planning, there must be consideration to the number of the children to have not to become a serious issue that might affect every

other plan in the family. The instance of having an attention to the number of the children however leads to the control in the birthrate. This can be adjusted through various measures that are ranging from both artificial and natural for the purpose. Before hand, people give birth the way they feel like, but the situation has shrinked the opportunity of doing so. However, at the point of looking at the negation of the economic instability, the issue of control on the birthrate might never be over emphazised.

42. Inadequate support and concern for the Intellectual management- in the situation whereby there is economic issues, the urge for the education of

both formal and informal are reduced. The pressure around makes virtually everyone to run towards the direction that can contribute or generate its economic benefit. The concern of the moment becomes the most essential need to the populace other than learning or looking into the information that can add values. Someone with the interest in the intellectual management concern must be able to create time for so doing, and this might be inconvient at the moment of having an un-ascertained future. Most of the countries in the world would have gotten to the peak but, the environment at which they operate had made their growth and development to be impaired and hindered. The set of individuals who have all it takes to leave and to carter for their daily bread do read, and sometimes fail to understand, not to mention someone that is not of the assurance of the days ahead. What I am insinuating is that, the environment at which one operates has a valuable contribution to the attractiveness of the intellectual management. Most of the student's are yet to be graduated and they are already thinking of becoming millionaires. There is nothing bad in becoming one if one can be constructive and reasonable to be one. Without information, there can never be re creation, without information there might not be an upgrade to the ageing way of handling issues. The information on both the formal and informal sector are however in association with the intellectual management, which means that, things that are not accessible physically can be rightfully accessed in the books and when one has the interest in reading. Good enough no idea or concept is wasted when they are fully exploited. Most of the graduates managed to complete their program just for the sake of moving above the poverty level, some only went to schools and institution just to fetch them job. At the point of having the programs, they often seek for the 'FOC' because of the issues that live around them which do not allow them to read or to have the sufficient reading ability. When the economy is adequate and conducive, more interest is given to the intellectual management which thereafter leads to the increase and productivity of such an economy.

43. Embezzlement and corruption- This is an act of misappropriation of fund. The money that is meant for the project and benefit of the others are translated to personal belonginess. People collect bribe before performing their function and lawlessness of all sorts. Minds and eyes are blind folded when the economic is not at peace. Though ordinarily, this should be very best condition to think vastly, but reverse

is the case in the African countries because of our nature and passion towards material things. It is even recorded that, some poeple are richer than their countries due to money they have embezzled. Economic instability creates a clueless economy and transforms virtually every one to lover of money never to be contented with what can give them their daily needs but to have thoughtless imagination on having everything. Sincerely, when one knows what poverty is, one will never want to experience it. If the government is findng it complex to attend to the issues of the society, the activities become the survival of the fittest. However, any slight means of having access to the public funds turn out to be the greatest opportunity for them to steal. Do not be surprise to be told that, many of the representative are earning vastly but the concern for tomorrow had turned them to thieves and corrupted individuals. So, to have an economy that can take care of the people and to experience development and growth that can lead the nations ahead, there is need to have competent hands, willing minds and those who have the interest of their follower while in their offices to be able to have economy that is stable, efficient and conducive for the attainment of the expected results.

There are many negative impacts that are injected into the society when there is economic instability and recession, but just to mention few, these points are enlisted. There will definitely be an upgrade to the points as time goes on to know the need to be extra ordinary careful at the moment of handling the economic issues mostly when we are privilege to serve in the public office or as representatives.

CHAPTER FOUR

EFFECTS OF EDUCATION

There are many relevancies that can be considered to be the advantage of education. This is just to have an overview of the realistic values that must be mentioned, some are well known while some are added. To be sincere, there is no limitation to the importance of the education because, the better one can see will definitely expand the facts one can measure up with. Education is light and power to those who have the dexterity to magnify the little they can learn, see or acquire. There is no doubt that education had made the world in which you and I are living to the taste of its nature and things that surround it. In a simple language, I will say that, education is the greatest accessibility to the realm of the unknown and the inspiration to the wonders that are yet to be visible, to create things that are known through the aid of the technology, innovation and creativity that are present at this age.

These are the considerations to my best understanding, while your logics and attestation that you can deduce from your thought are very valid in line with the effects of the education.

1. Ability to understand easily- What you know has an enormous advantage on your level of understandability. When you have been made to witness and to be availed with the information

through the necessary axis of acquiring knowledge, your understandability nature will be automatically intensively high. However, the ability to understand the issues and series of the problems in the global world is rested on how educative the populace is and the understanding nature of the human. Through education, understanding is enlarged and expanded to the level at which the activities are accessed and experienced in our time. In trying to compare what is happening now to what happened last ten years, you will definitely discover that many changes have taken place in term of various uses and application. This is an evidence of geometric growth that takes place when the education is counted relevant in the society. There will continuously be transformation and adjustment to the changes of the world, to be able to have the best of the opportunity and a system that operate at a very convenient manner. What are celebrated or counted most valuable now might not be notice in the years to come agenda.

2. Proactiveness- There are decisions that are very important to take place in life, and must take place if the world expect the necessary result therein. Knowledge is associated to the level of one's understanding and reasonability. All

what can be thought can be achieved if there is a focus on achieving them. Being able to manage the content of the mind at the specific period of their need to create a purpose that is required in their stages of priority is however termed to be proactiveness. This is an ability to understand the cogent need for an assignment or an action to take place. It is the ability to foresee the need to be involved in an action without being told. It is an agreement with the internal composition and innate man to have a physical exhibition of a view or idea. Proactiveness is when you know what is next without being informed or compel by any force to do it. It allows the system of the expectation to be in line with the plan to attain its significant value. It is a systematic approach to attain a goal or certain objective in their orderly manner. Therefore, having the qualitative education is the tool to have an unbeatable quadrant towards the best option of proactiveness and to have the advanced logical reaction towards issues that are made to be resolved, most especially in the economic deficiencies.

3. Bundle of insights are surfaced- When ones looks into the bundle of insights, he is trying to examine the things that the mind can construe or produce at a point in time. Cluelessness is one of the major

disadvantages of the ungrowing mind. Each one must have something significant he is thinking of or that can be seen at a point in time to be able to recreate activities that can envelop the human nature. Education should be the best avenue to be exposed to the various types of initiative and ideas that should make a significant contribution to the greatness of the humanity and the world at large. What one sees is quite different from what another man can see and so on and so forth. The ability to see the genuine fact in the education and to be unlocked leads to the substantial products that can be materialistic and that can lead to the development in all level. Education is an act of making one to realize that his presence in the world is clustered with opportunities and to understand that, without each one functioning at their respective realm and area of importance, their might not be result. Hence, the issue of having bundle of insight can not be toyed with at the time of extracting the effects of the education in the system of the world.

4. Economic repositioning-one of the major issue of the economies of the world is the issue of economic instability and recession. Many countries are living by the grace of God now as a result of the bad governance and the negative attitude of their bad leaders and

representative and the indecision of the followers to act accordingly to the paste of the development. There are various issues that emanates as a result of the inconsistencies in the leadership and followership of the world. Abject poverty prevails over a perfect living that should be in existence. Issue of the increase in the price of the products and living condition are not exempted in the context of the issue of the economy. However, the source of the repositioning of the economy can be ascribed to the level of the education and mental development that can be vivid in the operations of the system in the country or the economy in question. When a standard yard stick is to be in place, the nature of the education in correlation to such standard is quite very essential to make the reasoning around the development to be validated. One of the very essential needs of the education is very vivid in the state of the economy repositioning, and this might be formal or informal in nature.

5. Solution to the immediate and future problems- the problems of the world are enormous, and often they are the pilot to the direction at which effort and knowledge are excerted. Someone discovered the need to replace the old form of provision of light with bulb and florescent. Another man thought of connecting the world together in

term of communication with the use of the phone. A man initiated the computer to the existence for the conviniency reason. Another man brought the idea of making provision for easy transportation with vehicle, e.t.c. what I am trying to say is that, the pains or hardship that were passed through at a point or the other were made to be the sources of the solution to the immediate problems and gives the right of the order to think ahead. The problems in the years past are already turned to opportunity now, while the problems now are what create the opportunity for tomorrow. Solution is made for both immediate and future problems when the mind can trace the sources of such problems and can administer the need to have a quick solution to them. However, the reasoning of the people that are involved in the creation of the solution to the problems of the world is ordinary meant to be embedded on a solid foundation that might not be any other source than education. To be able to have a solidified planning that can attain the submission of the problems, there must be a standard education and information that can aid the power of thought to ascend to the height higher, and to have a meaningful contribution and perfect solution.

6. Provision of qualitative and competitive leaders and followers- in the midst of the unknowns, there are often leaders, so also, in the midst of the educated and elites. In the same way, followership exists in both of the group or nature of life. In the formal, the rules and regulation are well stated and written policies are made and so on and so forth, while in the later, there is nothing like written documents or policies. There is a usual saying that "where there is no rules, there is no sin" the kind of the leadership that are operated in the learned and educated forum are quite defined and well interpreted in their obligation other than the nature that are enclosed in the

midst of the unknowns. Do not forget our mission as regards the book work, we are only looking into the necessity of the education, either formal or informal. The followers that are educated are also very easy to relate with as leader, because, when they are introduced to the do and do not, they often observe them since they are documented. However, when one is looking into the provision of the qualitative and competitive leaders and followers, the issue of the education can not be exempted. Education brings about a harmonious relationship between the leadership and followership. It helps to understand the rules and regulation, and the conducts that prevail in a situation or the other in relation with the norms and values therein, and make the gazzate of the opertaion to be well followed.

7. Exposure-the grace to be availed the access to the things that are in operation from a spot to another, to know a bit of the culture and the behavioural pattern of a society or the other, to have an edge on the other in term of having the better knowledge of how something can be achieved or expressed in an advanced manner, and to have access to the opportunity and having the clues to the other issues around the world without being there is termed exposure. It is very necessary to be exposed before

something meaningful can be accomplished. One might not go to the school or the institution before being aware and having the due information that can make a significant impact in his life or in life. Exposure makes one to know the normalcy in the structure of life and the areas of adjustment. It makes one to be able to determine the areas of life that are meant to be upgraded and adjusted as a result of having comparism and contrast with what are happening in the globe of the world. To be exposed means having the large information that can be an added advantage to have an edge way on the others, to be able to reason with all what one has experienced to make an uncommon display and exhibition that is worthwhile in the environment at which one lives and in the world at large. Different things are always happening around the world, but it takes an educated person to be able to understand that which should be selected. Education is exposure, and it can allow one to have the right selection at the space of selecting the option to the increase.

8. Ability to be availed with the developmental concern- though without a formal education things can be created, but this might not be in the direction of the need of the world at the point of making them available. What one can see and act on within the time period of

consideration which can create comfort either directly or indirectly to the existence, and add value in its introduction is refer to as development. It is an increase that can be evaluated in both the physical and its contribution to the best nature and easiness that can be made available for the use of the world. Development can be accessed in the aspect of the activities and structure that can be seen and experienced while one founds himself in an environment. What I am saying is that, education and knowledge are responsible for the information that the mind can generate towards the developmental activities. What can be seen is quite essential when one is looking at what can be created. There must be a structure that can enhance seeing something that is worthwhile before the real nature of what mind has seen can be experimented. The way each man sees are quite separated, but out of all what men can see laid the development that can make improvement to their living and environment.

9. Logical and reasonable analysis and expression- when one says logical, one means that someone is coherent and uses common sense. It means consistency in disposition to introduce reality and something that has rational facts. Without a good thought and the ability to reason,

one might never be able to produce anything meaningful out of his system and reasoning ability. However, to be able to analyze oneself clearly and to have standard yard stick to the expression of oneself, there is need to have a basic education that can aid it up. Being logical means, being able to arrange one's thought and action to the tune of producing a resounding result. It is an avenue to have a structure that can produce what the mind could see, and what a man can percieve. It is named to be a reaction that is backed up with a resounding effects and acceptable outcome. The purpose of the education is to have an introduction to the indepth knowledge that are hidden and fine tuning them for the beneficial importance of the human, but some of the concept backfires at the point of having no resounding knowledge of placing them into the realm of their operation. Men can be reasonable to an extent when they are defending their impact or production of various activities around them, but the irony of it is that, most of the emanated concept that are not reasonable are the major causes of the trauma that are existing in the world. However, the point is to deliberate on the analyses and expression of the thought and action before they are made or undertaken, at the point at which they are processed and the result thereafter. To then have completeness of an understanding of the procedural contents, and to be connected logically and reasonably, education is very relevant.

10. Creativity and injection of innovation and technology- virtually all things were present in the last a decade have been transformed and changed to a better nature. I was studying the younger ones dancing sometimes ago, I discovered that, the young chap was only turning hands without the movement of his body, and yet, the dancing was fantastic and rhyme with the beat. Most of the old books read during our time were not found in the school curriculum anymore. There

was a time that the most expensive and the best car was beetle, peugeot, e.t.c. but the funniest aspect of it is that, if at all they are found now, they are limited in number. I will not forget the time at which we must queue up at the telephoning machine spot to make a call, also the use of the land phone stays fresh in my heart. There was a time at which trousers were made based on ¾, which means that, if you are not there, you are not attuned to the belief and norms of the time. To mention few, there is almost replacement for all the series of all forms of activities that were mentioned. What this simply denotes is that, creativity has brought about the innovation and advancement in the technology and thinking. Creativity has to do with the things that are attributable to the talent and trait. It has to do with the innate capability and structure of men. It is in line with what mind can access and to make out a unique output and action that are reasonable. However, being able to see without being able to act is one of the difficulties associated with the existence. Individually, many are pregnant, but only few can give birth to their babies, and sincerely, babies that are not born can not be counted as part of the existence. Resources are available but the use of the resources is not well defined. Most of the resources are disused and sometimes wasted unknowingly without understanding of what they are represented or their worth in their usage. Education can however give room to researches and findings that can increase the paste of the understanding of the men to know the products and the series of the associated resources, and to determine their present and future use and benefits.

11. Discoveries- discovery is very close in definition with the innovation and technology. Innovation has to do with the development or improvement on a certain issue which can be assessed in term of the technological application and its direct value after the discovery. It is an upgrade or increase in value

through educational acquired skills. On the other hand, discovery has to do with the knowing of the things are living with us but yet to be identified or things that are either in existence or supposed to be in existence that are yet to be proven or made to be. There are surplus of animals and plants that are not yet discovered, and these are meant to be available for the cure of an ailment, consumption as food, and for various puroses. When you discover, it means that, you are able to know what you have around you that has a purpose not define to the existence at the point of discovery. It means that, you are able to fetch the value in you out or determine that you have such content in you or your environment. Discovery leads to the creativity of the mind when a man subconsciously or consciously realizes that he has the evidents of authority to make use of what is discovered. Discovery allows the men to see beyond the level at which they can see, and know what they do not know but that exist either in them or their sorrounding. To however come up with the adjustment in term of economic stability and restructuring, creating of the additional value that can translate to the opportunity around the world might not be well over emphasized.

12. Unlocking of the internal hidden talent, skill and trait-Not to forget

the purpose of this book and the aspect at which we are relating on, we are looking at the impact of the education in the world system. One of the major contributions of the education is its value to unlock the internal man. There are many hidden talent, skill and potential in the men, but only few are used at the point of their usage. One can only make use of what he knows that are present in him or around him. The values and talents that are yet to be discovered are the talent and trait that are never used and they are very necessary to the enlargement of the world. To however tap into the use of the personal composition or to make use of the thousands of the uncountable talents that are yet to be revealed, there is need for such talents and traits to be discovered and to be identified. When talent and traits are identified, clues on how to make judicious utilization of the provision or available talent becomes a serious issue that must be verified. Hidden talents and traits might not be noticed without the help of the education and exposure. Because of the contribution of the education to the revealing and uncovering talent and potential, one can say that education is a significant part or an agent to unlocking the hidden internal talent and skill.

13. Full impact in the governance and political influences- Most of the African countries are experiencing various gaps and unhamonious relationship in the context of the economic performances. The governance and political consideration are meant to be structured on the solidified education for a better performance. To be able to see clearly the expectation of the populace and their needs, not only that, but to know how policies, budget, and various other essential components that make the economy to be well grounded are formulated and introduced to the system of the country, there must be need to have an education. Absence of education

is always very responsible for the shortcomings on the part to the greatness of the nation. What a man can see is very pertinent before one can relate on what a man want to do with what he can see. There must be adequate training that can lead to the greater performance and competitive nature of economy as a result of training and education in whole. To have an impacted government and political system, the structure on which they are erected is quite very necessary, and without having the total exposure to the demands of the system in which one finds himself, he might never be able to key in and to make a relevant contribution. Hence, the need to have an education of high value in the lives of the representative of the governance and the citizenries that aspires to lead.

14. Exposure to better techniques to accomplish task- without being able to try various measure of doing a thing or the other, one might not be able to come up with a substantial report or result of knowing the better way of handling such issues. There is need to have diversified ways of checking how best solution can be given to the world issues. There are numerous issues in the world, and often, they are resolved in different manner. But the best option to have a solution to the issues are always more important.

The tricks that however connote the efficiency to understand the various approaches are lured with the availability of the educational back ground. Education makes one to learn in each second, and gives one the right order to compare and contrast the option available. To however have a better technique to accomplish a task, there is need to have a meaningful attempt on different ways of dealing with series of issue, and thereafter comes with the quantitative and preferential result.

15. Instinct towards liberation and freedom- what this point is trying to illustrate is its function on the power of thought towards self liberation

and freedom. People tend to struggle for the avenue of being self reliance and liberated as a result of what they know and the exposure they are acquitted with. A solid reasoning and injection of value can add up to the level at which someone can think or the perspective at which he can reason to have a genuine libration. Just as it has been analyzed before now, education creates expansion and enlargement that can allow the thinking faculty of a man to be hyer-functional. Authetically, a lot of individuals are still living in the bondage without being able to determine or identify such condition. Education should be an avenue to be able to have a deep thought on the kind of the condition that one should operates on, and to have a well furnished and standard condition seen and created. When one can reason perfectly, he will definitely understand what he wants, and what he wants can be the ladder to the greatest height of his performance and maximum effort to attain the height of his expectation or directing his thinking and action, and gives him the yard stick that can take him along towards the accomplishement of his dream and creating a condition that is quite conducive for his living. At the instance of cross examining the the attributes or needs of the education, the instinct towards liberation and freedom must be part of its area of having improvement. The concept of freedom and liberation is traceable to the ability to know one's right and what belong to you. You must be able to say that, what you are defrauded of is yours before you think on the aspect of having it back. Freedom and liberation are the things of mind, and they are started right away from the inside mind of the internal disposition of the human. To have libration, there must be willingness to have it attained. There must be burning agreesiveness to make it possible because there is never a freedom that comes with ease, and there might not be any freedom that comes without having the freedom first internally. The funniest aspect of life is that, one might live through his life in bondage without realizing it. There must be light and authority to gain access to the beginning of the freedom which is its conviction before it can come into the reality stage. What you have that you know the important of having are what lead to freedom, not what you have that you do not know what they are to be utilized on. Not until a man can see the need to start up something different that can aid absolute freedom, he might never be able to experience it. Something must be responsible for the each action that man undertakes, without that, the aspect of the freedom might never be manifested. What arises the discomfortability within the system of men towards having an urge to have a condition that can lead to a more conducive nature of experience is essential to be examined before it is accomplished. There are a lot of things that must be considered at the point of looking into the need to have freedom, but sincerely speaking, educational importance is quite very precious among the factors. What you can see or think within you are the things that are relevant to what you want to be. The direct implication of this statement is that, the value of what you can see or experience at the point of checking the worth of living and expecting the transformation to an access of victory and a life worth to be experienced matters, and there might never be a meaningful information leading to a spectacular result without a tangible education and exposure to align one's path to greatness.

16. Self dependency and reliance- This particular instance is quite of the same nature with the just concluded point. When one looks into the aspect of liberation and freedom, it is more of looking at the physical aspect of life at the point of being not under the control of anyone, or being responsible for one's life without or little contribution or influence of another party. A country or group of people might come up with the mission of being

on their own or having the soveingty power to be self dependent or to control theirselves. Someone can serve a master for years, and after the service have a freedom as a result of having completed the term of the period of learning or being able to stand on his own. On the other way round, self dependency and reliance has to do with the ability to have the thinking of being on his own due to his priviledge to the educational background. There are thousands of the proffessional causes that are available in the schools that can be translated to the creation of distincted economic function. There are a lot of ideas that can be extracted from the surrounding to be made a greater opportunity in life. When one can create a unique idea, he is prone to having the perogative order and identification on such job. What I am saying is that, the capability of having the instinct towards the creation of the function that leads to the self dependency and out right reliance can not but be traced to the value or contribution of the education injected into the human nature.

17. It creates an avenue for now and future, and their benefit- Things change from time to time, I was trying to mention few of the things around while discussing on technology and innovation. What today needs is quite different from

what has happened in the years past. What happen yesterday might never be relevant to the issues at hand today, and what is happening now might be a pedentrial or foundational ground for what will happen in the nearest future, but not what will directly be needed. So, at the point of looking into the fashion and styles that has to do with the immediate desire of the wants and request, the nature of being able to access the information on what is happening or being able to read through what can lead to the catalyst of the transformation is very pertinent. Issue of now might be quite different from the issue of the future, but there will definitely be a learning point in the issues that are resolved now to have a better future. Looking into the benefit of the contribution of men, what we do now and in the future are attracted with the numerous benefits that might not be only view in the context of their functionality, and it is only those who can manage the future that are proned to better advantages when the future comes, and the future might be termed a minute ahead of your action. Education makes the evaluation of the effect of the men on the economy very realistic and measurable. So, to have a great value now and to be able to plan for the future event and purpose, there is need to have a good education and exposure that can propel the mind to the real needs.

18. It activates mind to success and greatness- there are thousands of definition that had been given to success and greatness. What is termed success or greatness by someone might not be similar to what you or another man had termed it to be. To me, the ability to see the genuine reason to keep on moving ahead for the accomplishment of a purpose by trying different categories of stylish ways of accomplishing and making impact that can transform the world and attract economic benefit while in progress is what I have termed success. I can term it also, as being

able to be connected with the path of the functionality that can add up values to one, and that which one has the apex degree of excitement and urge to under must accomplish. However, greatness is now measured in the level of one's accomplishment on his projected plans which anyway is the measure of his success. To be able to activate the mind in line with the success and greatness, there is need to be connected from within. There is need to know what exactly have you in mind, and how best it can be underlined to be monitored, and to have a constant evaluation on it. Having minded this, one can easily depicts his direction and the assessment in line with the quantification of success and greatness in association with the content of the provision of his target.

19. It gives sense of belonginess- Some people still wait for the others to initiate them accordingly to a certain conception or ideas. It is very possible for one to be the most important individual in life, and yet he does not know. Very possible to have what others are meant to count very essential and they may never be able to do away with in you or with you without being able to recognize it.infact, it can be your time to shine with what you can do, and yet you never step into the action that is at your arm's length to

be noticed. When someone is living in an environment without having a meaningful contribution or seeing the essentiality of his presence, it means he is not yet part of the environment. What takes one to belong to any area of life, is your ability to take part in the creation of the nature of the world that the entire people around the environment are willing to make or build. Without assigning any responsibility or obligation, one might not be able to easily identify his or her place of requirements.Majorly, the place of operation of human should be recognized by them, but in most cases, they are noticed by the poeple around them or the set of the individuals they work for or with. If someone is already having a purpose or task attained around you, and other several others are having other function accomplished without you having anything meaningful or assignment to accomplish, what it means is that, your purpose is important to compliment the effort available to create a substantial report and result, but one can as well conclude that, it is a confirmation of the awaiting opportunity that is yet to be utilized. Before a man can have a sense of belonmginess, there is pivot need to train the internal mind and innate man. A creative mind and willing mind is such a mind that connect human easily to the opportunities around them, and lead them towards the act of belonginess. A thorough education is however then crucial to have the mental sufficiency, to be relevant and to be able to key oneself in where and when needed without be compelled to doing so or with the little external effort.

20. It leads to creation of opportunities to the less priviledge- There is never any meaningful contribution of man to the existence that does not have something symbolic to contribute to the world. Creativity is an act of making possibilities to be opportunities. Opportunity is created by the input of the men or human. Anything meaningful done

with the intention of adding value to the others is as a result of creating advantages for oneself, and often, they are always the best measure to create substantial worth of innovation. Reversely, most of us think that being availed the priviledge to affect the others positively or to make them to grow is adding value to them but not directly adding the expected values to us. The fact remains that, anything that is actualized for the purpose of creating value or affecting others to be at their destination is an invested that might never go unfruitful or unrewarded. Either knowingly or unknowingly; opportunities are created as a result of the contributions of human being's functionality, and this creation often leads to the creation of the other opportunities for the less priviledges. Take for instance series of production by a well known businessman is creation of the opportunity for the others. Though, I have no statistic of the people in the Dangote Group of companies, but the fact remains that, thousands of the less priviledges are taken care of. The less priviledge does not mean the people that can not fetch for their living, but all the individuals that are either directly or indirectly engaged by the organization. More also, millions of the distributors and user of the roducts are also the benefial of the whole lots of the creativity. So, the better understanding of what you have in mind and bringing it into the manifestation creates opportunities for the others. Direct or indirect education is essential to the level of the performance of any set up one has in mind or on any economic activities that is set up, also, it gives the insight to not being self centred and to be able to covert the entire world to the arena possibility.

21. Good disposition is attained through the training and severe undertakings- The time that is invested in the training session or period to accomplish a particular knowledge is never wasted. There are numerous things that occur at the point at which one is trying to

attain the objective of knowledge acquisition which might not be directly dished out, but just mere information that can be very vital to a perfect outcome of a man. Part of the experience that can not be left out of the track to the attaining of the goal is moral and behavioural pattern. There are several lessons to be inculcated into the mind and the nature of who had gone for any form of training. The way one talks, relate with the world, how products and services are sold, making of business plans, looking ahead in the time of difficulties, e.t.c. are part of what is expected of any student that goes through training or any other individual that had gone for an informal training. While looking at this scenario, one can easily say that, learning of the disposition and training on the other moral values and experiences that should create one's life after living the training ground are available at the point of learning, which however makes education or its processings to have it very vital role in creating an economic of common sense.

22. It gives a discerning knowledge to the written laws and it appropriate interpretation- Writing of laws and regulation might be seen as an easy task that an ordinary person can do, but reverse is the case. Without being well grounded on the nature of the environment the laws and regulations are to be experimented,

or well nutured on the issues around the purpose of the emanation of such laws, one might never be able to conclude with a perfect nature of the rules and regulation that are worthwhile for its purpose.

Education is light. It gives better clarification of purpose and aids a quick understanding. So, writing of laws and regulation might not be accomplished without having thorough visit or impact of the education. Writing the laws and regulation is an aspect that should be peruse, another very ambiguous aspect of the laws and regulations is its interpretation. The laws and regulation must never be biased in its nature to have its mission fulfilled. Therefore, to have a complete laws and regulation, there is need to have those who are well grounded on the interpretation of the formulated policies available. Education however throws light and expands the understanding of the men on both the writing and interpretation of laws and regulation.

23. It reduces thugery and criminality- When one is exposed, there are some certain things that he will not do. There will be voluntary control at the instance of carrying out some certain function. I was once going through a path at my local area, and suddenly I meant with the set of the young boys smoking Indian helm. It was a raining day, and I was only

trying to manage the drain part of the land that connects to the major road, but three of them came to me to harass me, and asked me to go back. Sincerely, I could see that they were aggressive and on cheap drugs, and they can do and undo at the corner and in the dark segment of the area. I have to return back before having the consequence of it. What I am trying to say is that, education is very relevant in the life of human. There are some things that ordinarily, you need not to be told before you abstain from them. Though quite very annoying that at the present stage and age, most of the things that are not supposed to be done by the elite are more popular in their midst. The essence of the education is to have the priority schedule and to take decision on the do and do not. But when education is not made to be what it should be in life, or not attained in the light of its essence, its magnificient value in diminished. So also, the issue of reduction in thugery and criminality, when people are exposed to the appropriate pshycological contents of the education, and they are made to be well structured in it, they tend to give their priority to the things that are developmental and reasonable other than having their minds rested on thugery and criminality. Discovery of personal worth and potential can lead to growing a massive idea that can lead the entire world to the stage of greater fulfillment and having it might never bepossible without polishing the values in the human through education and its application.

24. It reduces chaos and economic unrest cum destruction in the environment- It is the busy body or less occupied person that are involved in the creation of chaos and unrest in the economy. When people have things to do, they are less aggressive. But in the absence of employment and good economy that can conceal the elements that are responsible for the disorderliness or causing issues unnecessarily, they misbehave.

Education should make life more meaningful and pleasant. Issues are meant to be leanrt on how best they can be rectified without being physical. Though, one might not be able to do away with such incidences when there is bad economy, and yet, the hardship aggravates. But there are better ways of handling issues other than causing chaos or unrest in the environment. Even, if there is need to have any demonstration or to do riot, there should be guide and prevention on the level at which such should be attained. We have experinced many riot and agitation that led to massive destruction of the social amenities and other provisions of the citizenry's benefits.

If these set of the individuals were able to identify those amenities as their own or for their personal uses, they might never be involved in destroying them. The logic is this, someone is made to be my manager, he took out of my resource to get me befitting furniture, but because of the misunderstanding between the two parties, I decided to set the furniture ablaze. Either directly or indirectly, I have wasted my resources. So, such is what is applicable to the destruction of the social amenities and other essential provisions for the citizenry use at the point of the unrest most especially by the blind minded set of the individuals. Therefore, education can be the best option to have a control and gazette on aggressiveness or griviousness if there is any in the economy.

25. Responsiveness to the problems and difficulties of the economy-There is no way there can be solution to the problems of the nations or economy issues without having the basement of knowledge. There is no economy without a single unit of issue, and sincerely, as one issue is resolved, another one arises. There must be a tactic that can create a value for the solution and remedy of such situations. Issues arise, and the solution is needed based on their emanation. There are some issues that have being from the time

immemorial, whereas some are created by the human and natural factors. The good thing about the issues is that, they are all proned to be resolved when one is predetermined to doing so. There is no issue that has ever surfaced without having solution to them when they become most critical issues to be generally examined and to have a lasting solution to them. There are series of different approaches that are available to put an end to the problems in connection with the relative issues around. And sincerely speaking, these issues are meant to be resolved if one aims at having a conducive nature of economy. There is no one without something to contribute at the instance of looking for the way forward at the cross junction of the economy epidemic. But only few are sensitive to the injection of these sets of the inbuilt characteristics to make a substantial effect. Different issues are handled in different way, and the procedure of the type "A" issue might never be what the type "B" issue is waiting for to have an edge way. However, my logic is that, out of these series of various categories of issues, it is essential to have an educational potency that can offer the best solution to any nature of their kind. This however takes us back to the topic, the essentiality of the education in the economy recession or depression. It can be said to be a source of creating a solidified solution to the menances of the world, most especially, the nature of the issues in connection with the discomfortability in the existence.

26. Vital avenues to connection- When one is looking at connection, one is looking into the system that makes something to happen and which eventually leads to another stage. Connection means being able to access the influences that are in alignment with the establishment of purpose and accomplishment of task. Before something can be referred to as being connected, there must be an association that is traceable in nature to their joint relationship. What connect a man to

another is different from what connect another man to another. In the chain connetion of life, some are connected by blood, that is being born by the same father, mother, friendship, working in the same organization, attending the same church or other places of religion, living in the same house, having shop or offices in the same complex, living in the same street,e.t.c. Sincerely, it has been proven that, all human are connected in one way or the other. Without connection, life can not be completed, because no man is an island of knowledge or an island of existence. There is no person that can run the activities of the life without having relationship with one and another. The president of the nation is connected to everyone because of the post he owns. The staffs of an organization are connected with themselves as a result of working in the same organization. Your mobile phones are connected together because they have unique features that are enclosed in the phones to receive reception to work interelatedly. So also, in term of existence, you and I are connected to a family or household either by both father and mother, father, mother,e.t.c. There is no one that exists without having a connection to a particular family unit. To however discuss on the connection in association with the education, one can simply look into the direction of having association with the right set of individuals, and the ability to have access to the nature of the advantages that can lead to transformation or completeness of change in any area of living. It is very possible that what one does is not as relevant as that of another man, and yet, he flourishes and blossom on it. When you are at the right place of the order, the difficulty not to have a complete demonstration of ideology and foresight is very dim. What I am saying in essence is that, your presence where your view is needed is attributable to the level at which you can operate. When one is with the right minded, and thinker, things go as if they are structured to move on without or with too much of effort. But when one is found at the other end of the side of the coin as a result of not being where he should or not being connected accordingly, reversed is the case. Well, my argument here is that, education can be a very essential element to the directional purpose and the type of the set of the individuals to be associated with. This however lead to the relam of connectivity and the height of viewing what should take place to move to another level

27. An avenue to expand in the scope of human thinking- Expansion in the scope of human thinking can be accessed in the various interpretations that one can offer. Its logical expression and his action

towards different specific associated function or activities of life. It is quite very possible for one to see something in his mind without being able to have a due clue to have various artilleries in operation to have a meaningful end result. There are many poeple with gigantic vision and dream that might never be accomplished. One is to have the power of thinking, and another thing is to be able to erect a solidified structure that can link the thinking to the global world operations. Without being able to think vastly, there might be difficulties in the aspect of being able to manage thought. A mere thought might be a mere vision that is impotent and lack of action.

Before there can be a speedy reaction on action, one's thinking must be able to transcend the mere thinking to have what one has in mind to be fully accomplished. If I may ask that, who does not need money, no one will say yes, and if I should have a million dollars looking out for who is in need of such, I believe everyone might be in need of it inclusive of the rich. So, what I am saying is that, if everyone wants to be rich or everyone is eager to collect money that the sources are not identified to them, then, everyone should know that, having money either as a gift or by one's effort has to do with thinking outside the box. Having the motive to have the money is the ordinary thinking while an avenue to making sure that you have the money is thinking vastly. With this illustration one can see that before crossing over to the realm of no limitation, there is need to have expantion in thought, and sincerely, no one might be able to have the due expantion without an adequate education. Education is so crucial in what the mind can think, and the management of the resources of the information.

28. Orientation and injection of value- to have a proper orientation and inestimable value, there is need to have a qualitative education either formal or informal way. Orientation means giving direction or expressing

the logic behind a certain circumstance to someone. Take for instance, when a new school boy enters into either secondary or tertiary institution, there is need to inform him of the various activities and conditions surrounding the institution's philosophy and code of conducts. Orientation is a means of addressing the need of the challenges and the expectation and the consequences in reation with the environment at which one finds himself. When one can not conceive an idea in the very well state, there is need to have an orientation that can instantly redirect such mind towards the essence of the idea and the intention. When there is massive failure of examination, the causes of the failure that are in connection with the inattentiveness to the instruction, reading or other factors can be examined by the teacher or guidance counselor not to have such menance repeating itself. Orientation can be pre-notification of the events that might occur or different things that can take place in the nearest future of journey or an attempt. At the other hand, injection of value can be considered to be the kind of activities that occurs to improve the worth and quality. When you enroll for a program, you have enrolled for the cause of adding value. When you are learning a specific job or handiwork, your intention is not to learn for learning sake, but to have something worthwhile extracting as value. In nut-shell, education makes one to have the approriate orientation and to be able to have a full injection of value that can extend the real view of a purpose to someone that is fresh to it or does not understand the whole requirement of it.

29. Exposure of hidden genius in men- Till now, we have several human with the series of values that are meant to be beneficial to the living and existence, but they are never in practise in any form or way. The most disheartening thing is to have something worthwhile for years of existence without it exploitation. There is no one without a

substantial value that should be a foundation to greatness or leading him to his destination. Hidden values are the hidden destiny, and hidden destiny is hidden future, hidden future is a covered development. Most of the nations are suffering of the depression and recession they experience because they have thousands of the able population doing nothing or being passive instead of being active in the economy activities. When the genius in men is exposed, they are always prone to libration and freedom we have discussed before now. Everyone has something so unique as said earlier, but the ability to unfold and uncover them leads to the attaining of a higher realm.

When one has something that is not in use, its worth having nothing. The possession of the inbuilt characteristics can only be appreciated when they can be dramatized and exhibited. Take for an example, you know how to play keyboard but you have decided not to play it, values are not what can be perceived without putting them into practices or exhibiting them. You must try all possible means to utilize what you have in you. You must be able to ascertain the trait that is in you to be able to effectively channel them to the places of their requirement. Education can aid up the discovery of hidden talents, and the genius in men. The essence of schooling is to increase one's knowledge or broaden oneself on the possibilities around. To know that all components of the wolrd are meant to define the accessibility to opportunity. It is said to be an avenue to introduce light in a gradual manner to the innate thought of men. Without formal education, a lot of the populace would not have been made. Also, in the aspect of the informal education, learning a specific job or the other is to groom one's internal tendency to do exploit. However, with the illustration given, there is always the need for the education to have an exposure to the hidden genius in men. Education wake the giants in men up and push them into action that can lead them to their greater desired levels.

30. Exposure to the world and how to blend with its activities- Blending with the activities of the world is very crucial to living. Life itself is a teacher, and everything in association with life should add value. There are thousands of activities in existence before we were born, some came up as a result of you being made, many are coming up as a result of our contribution and many even will still come up when we are no more. In the discussion before now, I tried to look into the aspect of uncovering the hidden genius in men. When hidden genius is exposed or

revealed, there is essential need to have it attuned to the activities around. One must be able to key in into the world and her activity. One must be able to discover where the genius uncovered can be dislayed and exhibited before he can turn them to the tools that can be relevant in the activities around. One gains experiences as he grows, what happens today might never be the nature of the experiences of tomorrow and so forth. These experiences should however be the factors to be made to key into the activities as one grows. In a systematic other, one can grow to experience various activities and yet, unable able to blend with the activities, but the quality of relationship that exist between life and proper education are more cordial to attain the highest degree of professional standard. Education can then however be termed as the releasing of the destiny and its directional focus towards the full exploitation and it capability to have a cordial relationship with the activities that serves as catalyst to changes and transformation.

31. Light, power, knowledge and signal to betterment- we have been relating on knowledge, its definition and interpretation all the while. The best interpretation that can be resolved at is knowledge being light, power and life. Also, if these qualifications are truly of best

definition to the knowledge, then, the issue of the betterment of life should not be exonertated. Light is for the illumination and clarity to have a better understanding of a certain issue or the other. Power is the ability to carry out a certain duty or the other out, or the ability to work, knowledge is information, awareness and facts. If these are the definition of the various words used, then their essentiality must be vivid in their uses toward their input into the betterment of the world. Construction of a structure and basement for the right living should be a simple thing. People should be able to think rightly and act rightly. The nature of the involment of the human should be positive and rational to dictate the conduciveness of the world. However, the impulse of the education has an enormous rate of value on the betterment of the future in a realistic objection to development and increase. Before one can see beyond the actual place of his performance, he must be able to go lengths to seeing the invisible. The spiritual realm of concieving a thought is relevant at the moment of execution. What one has in mind might not be fulfilled if one is out of it because, every other one might see the same thing in a different angle, and by so doing, what you have in mind might not be accomplished. But to come back to the issue at hand, rationally, all men should be very focused on what should translates to the betterment of the world, but pathetically, most of our input are injurious to the world. Education should be the best option to have a corrective measure and to fine tune the behavioural pattern of the world and to examine the nature of the best values that can be added to make the world better place. Hence, the need for the point mentioned as the opportunity of the education.

32. It is an authority to be in charge- When one says that education is an authority to be in charge, what does he mean? To be in charge is to be in control of the affairs around you. To be responsible for a particular

purpose or function. Having a legal back up or approval to carry out a certain duty or the other. A perogative right to act accordingly is a specific manner. Acting on a purpose officially or unofficially with the legal right or audacity to doing so. Being at the realm of the affairs to dictate and to control the activities to either suit the rules and regulation stated by the policies or to suit one's vision. Do not be surprise to seeing the gate man of an organization sending you back while you have something cogent and substantial to relate on with an organization, on several occasions, mere security men have stopped me or prevented me from gaining entrance into the organization.

What I am saying is that, the security are bestowed or conferred on with the authority to be in charge, though they might not be acting legally or incorrectiveness to the instruction given. So, to cross examine the education in relation to its function and essentiliaty, one can say that, it does make one to have the strenghtability and courage to be in charge and to defend one's action. When you are enlightened, there will be thorough coordination that must avail you the authority to be in charge. Without both formal and informal education, the issue of the common sense to be in control might be far fetched. So also, when one is relating on the impact of the education on the economic growth and development, the citiszenry must be able to access the authority to be part of the development and the necessary adjustment.

33. It unlocks internal mind to decide- Decision on what to do or not is very compulsory at a point in life to move ahead. Mostly, when one has numerous intentions in mind, there is need to analyze how important they are to be able to tabulate them in their hierarchy of preverence. When one can not decide, he does not set for moving head. The decision of today is the true nature of what a man will be in the nearest future. To have a competitive decision in the future, there is need to be able to fine tune one's

thinking and realizing the importance of the needs or desire. Decision that is meant to be taken today should not be left till next day else, it might lead to no decision. One of the most sensitive areas of life is the time of taking decision and moment of acting on the decision. Good decision should be taken to be able to have good ending and result. Good decision is subjected to what man has in mind and how best he can utilize them to create the expected result. Things that are common to the internal mind are very critical, and they are in association with what a man can see. A reasonable man must know what he wants to embark on before making an attempt to doing so.

Human beings do not just do something because they want to do it, there must be something to be derived before a decision is taken. Mind is contained with various decisions which can either be good or bad, but the decision to make use of the information or thought in either of the two ways gives the definition of such a decision. Human being must be in control of his mind to checkmate the wrong decision and encourage the right decision. However, the decision is however for each individual to either accept what is good or not, to do a certain thing or not, and that is what is referred to as choice. You can take a choice that is quite different from mine, so also I can otherwise. In relation to the topic at hand, the nature of the information you can access or you have in you can be the best producer of your thought and action. And frankly speaking, the exposure you have connotes how vast you can be in the aspect of decisioning. Therefore, education can be of assistance to the greatness of the production of the information that the mind can release for the use of the human function.

34. It is a signal to inform us all that we have all it takes to have solution to issue around us- I must have said something of this nature in a part of this book while addressing the importance of education. There are issues all around, even when there is

no issue, the injection of the human efforts create one. If there is no issue to be resolved in life, I want to tell you that life can never be meaningful. The prevailing issues make the living to be enjoyable and lively. This is what makes us to think beyond what we can see, and see what ordinarily we should not have seen. When issues are not well managed they are destructable and haphazard to the growth and development of an economy. But when issues are well managed, they are always the avenue to grow beyond the stage at which one was before deteting the issue. Issues make the mind and the brain to work in an exceptional manner. No wonder one dude said that, you may not have common sense not until you are left with nothing. The illustration of this statement is that, when one is comfortable, he might not find the reason to think beyond what he can see, but when things get disarray, human thinking turns multiple to find solution. With the expression, I am only saying that, solution around us might not be handled diligently or with passion if the education back ground of the people involved is not comprehensive. Education often allows us to see what is wrong, and not only that, but to profer solution to what is wrong. Education is an indicator or signal on the imperfection of life, when something needs an adjustment, there is always a flashing light on such issue in the mind till it is resolved. Hence, the need for the education in the lives of the global populace, and to be the best ally in the societies for the better days to come.

35. Creation of identity and brand- When one has been able to discover the hidden genius in him and he can apply them accordingly, the identity is already in place. Two people can have similar view but at the point of experimentation, they might never be similar. This is because of the human difference, except they copy themselves. Also, being an identical twin does no mean that you are the same in the real evaluation of life.

The point at which what you can see turns out to what you are doing creates the true nature of your mind to classify your identity and brand. To be able to have completeness in the brand and identity, there is need to have the educational input to analyze the brand and identity in such a way to make it more easier to the world to understand the nature of the business and activities you are into or that you do.

Identification and branding can however be said to be the varieties of products or services that an organization is involved with. The number of the activities however depends on the strength of the business or how diversified the management or the sole proprietor is made up. Take for an example, a dry cleaner of cloths should be able to tell us that, he is into washing, ironing, starching, pick up and delivery, e.t.c. this illustrates the various activities that the organization does in a few words and gives a better package for the identity of the organization which in returns relate on the improvement either directly or indirectly. However, the effect of the good standard and the operation of the witty industries are very essential to the nature of the economy that can be experienced.

36.   Creation of fame and popularity- sincerely speaking, fame can be created in any way. I once learnt of

a man that jumped into the lagoon just because of an issue or the other. Though, the logic was childish and somehow illogical, but the deed had been done! And I must sincerely confess to you that, the man that was not known for years was known by the entire Nigerian within twinkling of an eye. If possible, I guessed he might still like to live on after the incident. So also, we have series of individuals that are famous suddenly without any stress or difficulties on their part. But the ideology of the book is centred on a reputable fame and popularity that can be seen in the convergence of the products of the education. There are some fame that are negative in nature, such as the enumerated examples, but to be frank, there are fames that can be built in logical and responsible way through the introduction of what someone has to give. What a man gives should be the true carrier and builder of what he should be or the kind of the fame to be madeup with. The uniqueness in the attributes in association with the nature of human should label diversified fame that should differentiate one from another. Talent and trait are more disciplined and suggested to be the avenue to create greater thought, vision, purpose and impact. To however have such a creation of fame and popularity that is recommendable in line with the provision of this book, education and exposure to series of information that can lead to the apex level of creativity is extremely demanded.

37. Exhibition of possibility- Exhibition of possibilities means the series of the nature of approches that come together to demonstrate the possibility of accomplishing a certain project or purpose. There are several theories that have been propounded based on the testings and verification in both formal and informal apparatus which strictly relate to the possibility of the events. Someone must have tested that honey is good for cuff. Another man must have come up with the use of bitter leaf for something that one might not even think of. There

was a time someone came up with a funny but real theory in the LUTH at the time of EBOLA disease outbreak , that "Ewedu and Amala" are good cure of the disease as at the time. What I am saying is that, often at times, most of us think very far away as regards what can be the solution to a problem or the other without verifying or looking into the use of the things around us to create possibilities. There was a time that the idea of the pure water was not in existence, people never knew as at then that, they can generate their income on the making of the pure water or perhaps, they were living in the crude way of selling ice water, but suddenly, someone came up with the idea, and many other individuals immediately imitated him. This must have changed several lives to a better standard of living. When something is backed up with experimentation, poeple tend to have all it takes to be able to quickly reason along. Some poeple needs other to start up something before they hijack such project from them. They might not be able to see or have any motivation to doing something, but immediately they are priviledged to gain accesss to what someone else does, they build their structure which might be more stronger than that of the initiator. Gone are those days when I was still battling with the acquisition of my certificates in the university, I have a friend that forgets easily what he reads, but as soon as he is able to look into a point on your script in the examination hall, the kind of development he will give will be much more interesting and loudable than what the initiator of the point gives. To round up this point, I want to say that, the possibility in life is in relationship with what is known. When one is widely exposed, he will definitely often be in the alignment with the possibilities of life. I have not said, having a break through is easy, but the ability to conceieve the possibilities of life is quite very necessary to be able to attain the hieght of one's destiny and the realm that is in concordance with what one is connected with. However education in either the formal or informal is very necessary to be connected and to have an end result to the possibility of life.

38. Directional purpose on the head way to greatness-there is different between having being able to discover oneself or to unlock one's destiny and the directional measures towards the accomplishment of the pretangential purpose. When one catches up with an idea, he knows what he is willing to do, but the intention might never be accomplished without having a solid planning and steps that can lead him to the purpose. If greatness is by what you can see or talk about, then, I think there will not be any

one empty or in need of anything. Greatness is the ability to work in line with the provision of the purpose to attain it. These are the structures that are laid to have systematic movement till the mission is fully accomplished. The standard is that, one should be able to have a directional plan that can translate vision to mission fulfilled. This often entails having different types of plans, feasibility studies, development plan, e.t.c that are meant for the practicalization of the objective. Without a solid plan, a project might flourish for a while and thereafter collapse. We have many organization that were able to be known for just few months or years before they went to the state of extinction, and we have many that have been in existence for years, and they still flourish at the greater height even while the economy is not suitable. A solidified plan makes one to be well nutured on the approach to be made to switch over at the point of the need for adjustment. That is when one is talking of the adaptation or adjumnental values to the situation. There must be a plan, and the plan must be well attuned to the developmental purpose of the real intention of a man. A purpose without a plan is a purpose without an edge way and ending, and this might lead to the collapse of such intention. Therefore, the need to have a very rugged mind, and above all to have a significant plan that can create opportunities and stand as foundation of intention to be real and to flourish in term of its accomplishment.

39. Qualification and certificates- What this is saying is that, as soon as any one is exposed to the education, there is always qualification and certificates that backs up the fulfillment of the knowledge acquisition or the course. At this junction, I am not looking into the acceptability or inacceptability of the certificate, but looking into the demand that moves with the accomplishment of learning mission. Though, we still have many organization, industries, place of

work,e.t.c where after learning, mostly handiwork, certificate are not given. But the number of the ones that issues out certificate outsmart the ones that do not give certificates at this dispensation. Being able to be priviledged to be exposed to the education means, having the access to the certificate and qualification. Many have different nature of degrees,TC,NCE,B.SC,MBA,M.TECH, M.SC,HND,ACA,ACCA,REFRIGERATOR SERVICE MAN,MECHANIC,CAPENTARY,HAIR DRESSING,TAILORING e,t,c. the advantage that has been given by the qualification is in association with the opportunity the education extends to them. So, to have a good qualification and certificates, there is need to be attuned to the education and to be learner that is often willing to know more about the solution to the living problems.

40. Communication in official languages- In the school, the official language is very compulsory and made to be the major language that must be adherent to within the vicinity of the school environment. Though, someone like me was unlucky to have gone to the school whereby we speak our dialet or languages, but at the later year, were able to get adjusted gradually to the official language. Communication in an official language makes one to relate in an

official manner, it has to do with the world class nature of doing things. Teachings in the schools are done in official language, meetings of all kinds are done in the various organization in official language, transactions around, mostly by different tribes and citizens are carried out because of the language difference in an official language, examinations and interview are often done in an official language,e.t.c. education creates an avenue to have all what it takes to be audacious in communicating, mostly in the official language. Since the consideration of the book is rested on the importance of the education to the improvement of the economic instability and recession, the informal sector can not be exempted. I can attest to this, most of the mechanics around my working place while I was still in the financial sector can communicate with the official language. Though, some communicate in an appaulling way but some are completely fluent. Most of them would not have found it easy if not because of the work they do and the kind of the elites they relate with. Since education is transmitable, the ideas in it can be learnt outside the four corner of the wall of the school or through working. Most of the house boys and house girls did not know how to speak in an official language before they are employed, but their relationship with the household in which they are employed changes their content. Most of them speak official language as if they have gone to learn it. Therefore, to mention the opportunities that are in correclation with the education, the aspect of the communication in the official language must never be ommitted.

41. Ability to relate with the other part of the world- If we agree with the advantages to be availed with the dynamics in the official language, then, interpreting the relationship with the other part of the world might be very easy to examine. There are different types of the approved official languages with

their member states. English language is for the Britain, French is for the France, German is for the Germany, Arabic is for the Arab, Spanish is for the Spain, e.t.c. Anyone that can speak any of the languages among their member countries will without no doubt be able to   communicate easily on any related issues with their other counterpart from the same continent. Transacting on the business consignment and activities might not be difficult to do. Bilateral relationship among the countries will be very easy. Also, the issue of formulating of the rules and regulation governing their relationship might not be difficult to sort out. In the same vein, the interpretation of the regulation will be very easy to do. To curtail our explanation on this important relative issue on importance of the education, one can conlclude that, without an education there might not be coherent relationship among the nations.

42. Creation of good manager and manegarial skill and contents- Without knowing the worth of what you are engaged with, you might not know the reason for you to manage it appropriately. The value of what you do or you are engaged with in life should introduce the need to be a viable manager. When one is responsible, he knows what responsibility means. A mind that is

well fine tuned can be the manager with the full of series of dexterities for the dynamics of the economic importance. One must be well grounded and well thought to know what management meant. There is no amount of money given to you as a person that can not be extincted when you do not have the knowledge of management. There is no one that can be good to work with you or that you can work with when you do not know what management of the people means. When you do not know how to go about doing what you are involved with, there might be ambiguity to have a proper management. Education is the source of many insight that acts as catalyst to the greatness and advancement of many companies, because, the life of the business is in the kind of the policies and ambition of the organization,and how effective the management is. To however have what it takes to have a good manager and managerial skill, one must have been learned or passed through the drilling phasses either formally or informally, this is what education refers to, and what it contributes to the reshapening of the mind and personality.

43. White collar job creation- There is no doubt that the incumbent major work or secured job in the world are the white collar jobs. Though, this is only attributable to the formal

education. Most people seek for jobs and they are gainfully employed, many are still looking for the openings while thousands of the younger ones in the institution that are yet to even start the journey are eying white collar jobs advantages. The adverse effect of the white collar jobs can not be excluded from the different form of issues that various economies are witnessing or having at the moment. It creates jobs, but such jobs are often not symbolically productive in nature. These natures of jobs are banking, insurance, brokers, clerks, secretary, typist, name every other work that are secured with certificate or based on one's skill. Though they are very relevant in the aspect of grooming the economy, but they are not directly productive in nature. Most of the people that are working in such an organization are working based on the instruction and policy, and basically because of the renumeration. This nature of jobs are often robotic in nature, and might not require one to make use of his initiatiave or discretion while handling them if one has not attained the managerial level. But the advantage is that, it creates an avenue for many individuals for their livelihood, and its affects their standard of living in a way or the other.

So far, we have discussed on the need to be exposed to the education and to be well nutured before there can be transformation in the economy of the world. We have seen that, there is no hope for any nation that has made education not its primary duty and one of its most essential concentration or focus. Apart from all that has been enumerated, there are other great importances that can be viewed, but for the cause of this book, at the time at which I was looking into the pivot factors that education gives, I was only able to think into the areas enlisted. There will definitely be adjustment and ugrade in the book as time goes on to be able to make it very adequate and friendly to all season as it might be through more of the information I can extract, and your views and suggestion. Education is life and it is a pivot aspect that the entire nation must never handle with levity.

CHAPTER FIVE

INHIBITING VALUES TO EDUCATION

Since the importance of the book is not in relation with the inhibit values of the education, but the importance of the education, I will not be able to talk at length on this particulr part. Though some point will be enlisted, but there will not be too much of explanation towards them. Hopefully, there will be another book that will relate on the sub topic in the nearest future.

INHIBITING VALUES TO EDUCATION

*Mind set- This is the nature of mind one possesses. It has to do with what someone has concluded that he is doing or want to do. It has to do with the state of mind towards a particular action or activities. Therefore, if one has the wrong mind set, there might be difficulty in achieving or having the necessary education.

*Unwillingness-Being willing is having interest in something. When you are willing, there might not be any form of force or compelling act to do what you are supposed to do. Things are done freely at the point of willingness and there is always the urge and the need to be self motivated to accomplish such task. So, when education is not done willingly, there might be issues to have it attained.

Arrogancy – Some people find it very difficult to learn from the others. Humble mind is such a mind that can habor information and learn. Education is subjected to various areas of life, and it can be accessed in anyway, and this can be when one is very humble. There are a lot of things that would have changed many people's life but because they are arrogant, they are never mindful of such crucial insight. There must be a tender mind before one can learn.

*Detest to rules and regulation and order- When one does not know how to stick to the rules and regulation, how to adherent to them, it becomes a serious issue for him to learn. A learning mind should be a respecter of the rules and regulation. One might not be able to learn without having the disposition of being able to attend to the rules and regulation in a perfect order. You must be a reasoner and one who obeys the policies that are guiding the area at which you operate before you can be able to click into the learning phase of life. There must always be a code of conduct that must be attuned with at the point of learning, and such must be strictly followed.

*Attitude and character- In term of attitude and character, I meant that, one's disposition must be able to comply with the environment of learning. This is what leads to the aspect of being able to comply with the rules and regulation. The attitude and character must not violate the policy of the area of learning if truly one needs to learn. Learning has to do with how one can represent himself in term of his behavoural character. A good attitude and character are demanding for a learning efficacy.

*Laziness- most of the people are always very lazy. I have been able to meet with the poeple who say that I can not read anything that is not in common with the academics books. What they meant was that, without having anything that has to do with examining them for qualification reason or for upgrade at their places of work, they do not have the time to read any other materialistic documents. People read for the sake of having a good qualification and upgrade, not for the sake of developmental purpose and expansion in the context of reasoning and its application, mostly, during the tensed economic situation. There is a common statement in the school then, that if it is not read to understand, it must be read to pass. Most of us only read books to pass. Any reading that is not relevant to the examination in the institution is counted irrelevant and not substantial. There must be urged for the information that can add up value and exposure to the minds of the individual and their thought.

*Inability to discover one's purpose- When purpose is discovered, one can be able to have what it takes to build enlargely on it. Without the understanding of purpose there might not be ability to learn accordingly. There must be a purpose, and the purpose must be made to be developmental and growing in nature. When a purpose is seen as developmental and growing in nature, it attracts learning to be part of it to materialize. Discoverying of purpose is disoverying of the essentiality of education.

*Discouragement-when one is discourged on a particualr purpose, he might not be able to learn any more. When discouragement set in, there is always an obstruction to learning. Stability in the state of mind has to do with the height of having the capability to learn. Learning is a technique that has to do with how stable one is, and how one assimulates. There is never the grace to assimulate or harbor information at the state of being confused or not having the stable mind. Discouragement is seen as a factor that might inhibit the education when it is possessed or formed to be part of human.

Eagerness to make money without investment- There are thousands of youth and people that belive in the life style of making money without having anything to do prior to making their money. The law of nature states that, there is no food for the lazy men, but quite very pathetic that, more are available for the the lazy men than the hardworking beings now. The Holy Book also affirmed and confirmed it that, in your labour you shall eat. But to the surprise of the activities around, people do not give attention to the making of money anymore in a judicious and logical manner. When there is urged to make money ordinarily without having the due procedural ways, there is every tendency of losing the interest in the education which can be asterisk as part of the major concern for the improper or deffect in the education.

*Unscrupulous mind or cheating- Just as examined, when there is feeling for the cheating or defrauding of the others, and there is no effective laws guiding it, this might lead to lawlessness which improves on the laziness of the cheaters and even encourages others to be involved in cheating others. When the law and regulation are not solid enough to manage the human behavioural pattern or to check mate the attitude of the citizenry, they count education to be worthless or relevant to be embarked on. The mind that learns does not think of the loop holes of the others to cheat them, but looks into the loop holes of the others to make provision for the corrective measures that can assist their weakness and make them, and through it, to become the avenue to make an end means.

*Financial constraints and incapability- When one finds it difficult to eat or does not have money, it might be a detterent to a proper education. Gone are the days that education is free, one will be in the school, and the Government will be very responsive to all form of requirement ranging from food and other material things, text book, note books, e.t.c. Reverse is the case now, in the sense that, there is no provision for absolutely free education. Thousands of the tomorrow leaders are found on the road at their tender ages selling or hawking commodities to survive. At the present age, we have some private schools that have their school fees at an amount above a million of our currency. The point remains that, someone that does not know what to eat in the morning or that does not even have any plan yet for his future might not consider what can not fetch him money immediate as important need. Often at times, the so called handiwork also requires one to pay for the graduation or make a presentation for the appreciation of the boss. In similar case, the tools, implements and other necessary materials that are meant to be purchased after graduation are subject to the consideration of the mind before moving into any form of apprenticeship. When there is no money, there is always no tendency to accomplish in term of investment into the future through education acquisition.

*Inability to be prepared adeqautely for learning-Being inadequate to prepare for the learning means that, one is not informed of what education means. Before there can be learning, there must be submissiveness of mind to view the issue to be considered at the angle that one does not know anything about it. Not that you do not know, but to be able to extract values from the others or to learn, one must be humble and be very inquisitive to what the other person who can be a teacher, boss or any other individual as viewed by you is willing to express or come up with. There are always rigors in the learning of something new and sometimes, something old, and without being able to overlook or cross over the rigors, there might never be solution to the intent of such an individual that considered learning. Simplicity allows one to learn a new trick other than the trick he is accustomed to. It makes one to have bit of the experience of how others feel about a related issue or knowledge about other things. This is an avenue at which spirit is kept away from all what it has acquired to look into how more can be learnt and be part of its value. However, at the attempt of doing this, there must be preparedness for the difficulties and all other factors that might be noticed as detterent to accomplishing the set goal or purpose

*Distraction-There are lots of distractions that can be mentioned to be an inhibiting

value to a resounding education. Too much of all things are very divastating to life. We have mentioned a lot of distraction while enlisting the points, but other distraction to be mentioned are, too much of social life, too much of passion for money, too much of irrelevant things as associated to you and I, bad gangs, inability to have a proper schedule for different issues of life,e.t.c. When there are alots of distraction, there is always every tendency to have minimal acquisitional enablement to be able to admit education into one's system. Distraction must be well dealt with to have an operational active human composition and a willing mind.

*Lack of courage- When one is in absential of courage that he can achieve something worthwhile undermust, it becomes a very great issue to have advancement, most especially in relation with the empowerment through education. Apart from the school education, we have other vocational training and teachings that are to introduce people to the field at which they can fetch their daily income and earning, but yet, many people consider them as no way, possibly because they have a good certificate from the great institution or because of their unwillingness or perhaps because they have lost interest in what such can offer. Without the courage that something substantial can be the end result of investing into the education, there might never be courage to experience it. Even in the formal education, it is obeseved that the courage is lost in the sense that, before the completion of the programs in the tertiary institution, students' tend to have the organization of their preference to work or apply to work instead of looking at what they have to give independently or to offer the existence. Education should be a factor to an expansion and self reliance, to be able to create things that are crucial to the remedy of the existing condition and circumstances. However, courage is demanding for the acquisition of knowledge and reformation of the mind that can make a substantial impact in the society and the world at large.

*Exposure and the area of upbringing- The area at which one is born and grown might have a negative or positive contribution on how one feels about life. The behavioural pattern of those that are in existence in your surrounding and the nature of the information you have access to contribute to who you are at the moment and in the nearest future. If one is born in the bush and he has not been able to have access to the due information around him or that can create him, what creates him might be limited to the refrained opportunity around him. There must be exposure, there must be movement, there must be information that can make the people to discover themselves without too much of words of admonision. When the exposure is real and the area of the upbringing is averagely conducive, people can easily grow themselves to their taste. And at the very stage or state of making provision for this, no one can do away with education. The act of building and constructing one's life to his taste with the use of the information and knowledge around him is called learning that can be simply reffered to as an education.

*Bad governance and political instability- Sometimes, the set of the things we quote are never supposed to be the value that should distrupt one while aiming at a focus. One's focus is meant to be very enabled and strenghtful compares with the difficulties around them. To be frank, the issue of the political instability and bad governance should have been the best avenue to attain greatness if it has been critically examined. This is because of the consideration that, the numbers of the issues are the numbers of the advantages of the solution that is needed and that can be provided. Such that, when there is any issue, there should be an advantage in connection with it. But sincerely, reverse is the case. Many think that, the nature or state of hardship or inconvinieces should be the state of making money or being aggressive to material things. When the future is not well interpreted, identified or ascertained, only the positive thinkers and the executor of the necessary adjustment to the future can be relevant to have a meaningful impact to be able to key in. However, on the education, instead of having acquisition of knowledge, the most prevailing option is the zeal and passion to the juvenile delinquencies and various atrocities. The masses tend to shift their mind away from the importance of both formal and informal education to the irrational thinking that often generates income in an easy manner when things are going wrong most especially through the interference of the government.

Bad orientation-when the knowledge of something is not enough or there is confusion on the part to fulfilment, there must be a counselor to admonish on the way forward. The nature of the counsel that one receives matters at the point of having a mission fulfilled. One must be able to know that, not all information is necessary to the completeness of the fulfillment of the vision. The nature of the orientation that one receives matters, and the way the information are implemented are quite very expedient also. Some people are often having ill luck as regards the information they can access at the point of having issues, while others are very lucky to have perfect information that can translate their wishes to the best of luck. At the point of making decision on what should be the way ahead as regards the constructive aspect of life, a good orientation is very pertinent to be able to see the need for such investment. The nature of the orientation might depict the value someone gives to the education. Most of the younger ones that are meant to be engaged are not, because of the information that is absential to them. I have met with various set of individuals with vast reasoning and very widely knowledgeable but yet, they are never availed the greatest priviledge to be made. I quite agree with the statement that says that, "you are the architect of your future" but sincerely, many would never have been priviledged to attain the height at which they operate if not because of the information they have accessed. So also, I will like to buttress it that, a good orientation should be made available to the growing ones and the entire populace to make best use of their opportunity.

Wrong application of religion-very sure many would have seen this point very not too logical or alarming to the hindrance of the education in the world, but sincerely, this is one of the issues that have been from time immemorial. The first thing that came to my mind is the issue of not allowing the growing ones to have a proper education because they are supposed to be learned on the religious studies. The growing ones should be availed the opportunity to have the access to the series of information that can create them or reform them. I have not said studying the principles of religion is not proper or neccessary, what I am saying is that, there must be a wider avenue to receive and to interprete the words in the Holy book. Without a proper education, it might be difficult to read through the whole ideology of the provision of the religion in its application to the present world. Things are changing, though the words of God remains valid every day and always, but the application of the world of God to the civilization and the knowledge that can make conducive environment should not be ignored. No wonder, there have been tremendous killing and wasting of lives irrelevantly. An uncivilized mind might not be able to know how best to persuade the civilized minded on how to accept his phylosohy or idea, than to be violent in his attempt. Civilization should make one to understand that though the leaders of the religious were not able to go schools because there were no schools, but if they are in the system now, they would have attained the greatest of the level of the academics. They were absolutely educated in the sense that, though they did not attend any institution, but yet laws and rules that are unbeatable till date were formulated by them. The other consideration is the lack of knowing that vocational jobs are availing the congregation the information that can add up meaningfully to them is an avenue of making them. Some religion centres do not believe in empowering the younger ones around them, neither do they avail the younger ones the right of the order to have information that can transform their lives. They believe that, they are the only ones that have something to offer, whereas if only they can be silient, they will definitely see more of the better standard and the yard stick that can elevate their ministries and dream. The sincere part of the life is that, what you have might not even be useful for those who are with you, but of extremely need by those you can not identify. Information and knowledge are meant to be allowed in the midst of the congregation to add value to them. The most annoying thing is that, the congregation are defrauded of what they should know or what should have enlarge them, and yet, the religious centre demand exceedingly for different collection and their tithes. When poeple can see clearly the major reason for them to learn accordingly and to experiment their dexterity, they can either consciously or subconsciously awaken themselves to develop the giant in them. The attitude of the religious centre must be controlled to make education relevant and impartational to the people they lord or shepherd.

Hopelessnes-when one does not know what it takes to live his life, it becomes an issue for him to interpret things that are demanding to uplift him to the height of greatness. Issues occur day in day out, but the ability to manage issues are what creates the hopefulness in the hopelessness state. When one has not considered anything meaningful to be benefit of his living or has not been able to determine what existence is all about, or thought that it is impossible for him to have edge way amidst the tribulation and storm around, he is led to the state of hopelessness. Hopelessness is the state gloominess and a state of inability to access what life has to offer to oneself. When one operates in the realm of this nature, he tends to be oblivious of the intricate values of the existence, decide to live his life as if it is not valuable to him. To have a broaden knowledge that can operate at the height of being congnizance of usefulness of education in life, the state of mind must be hopeful and expectant. Hope is the assurance of what you have not seen or have not experienced, but having the due thought that, it shall manifest. The manifestation of hopefulnes is what translates to fulfillment and success. Therefore, there is need to have a due hope for the prospect in the education and to have the passion and zeal to be developed therein.

CHAPTER FIVE

CONCLUSION

Very sure that the issuse considered so far are not new to anyone, they are very simple issues and they have been from time immemorial, but till now, the issues are not yet to be resolved. The kind of the issues faced in a society are different from themselves, and also, they issues are not similar to themselves in term of the existence on daily basis. What happens today might never be what happens tomorrow, and that of tomorrow might never be the issues that will exist in the years to come. This is the reason why, the population should be dynamic and grow with the society in which they have found themselves. Prevailing problems are not supposed to be unresolvable in nature because, any problems that are not resolved are the problems that exterminate the tenacity to make a reasonable impact and to grow.

Mind you, there is no perfect economy, and there can not be any. But there can be a perfect solution to the issues as they arise. The efficacy to proffer a standard solution to the exsiting issues of many developed nation had made them to be growing economy. When issues are unending and unresolved and yet, other issues are adding up, there is always complication at the point of visiting them or acting on them. Things that should be able to strengthen the growth and development in the economy are very essential to have an economy at her best nature. Most of the leaders in the democratic nations tend to fault other leaders of the defects in the economy. Though, it is real, but the work to do or the impact to make should be more significant compares with the flimsy excuses.

However, every one should be directly involved in the issue of the building of the economy. There is no one without something substantial to contribute to the economy growth and development. You should not be compelled to act accordingly, neither should anyone should be waited to have directory or force before making a reasonable contribution.

The most essential aspect that the book is centred on is however on the significant of both formal and informal education and their chief contributuion to the economy advancement.

Education leads to major translation and transformation. It means that, there is no change without the necessary contribution of the education. Education makes it more easier for the nation to see the need to grow, to formulate the policies and tricks that can cause a turn around and that leads to improvement in all sectors. If education is not a dedication towards the growth and development, the various contribution that should give birth to the advancement and increase work against the nation unknowingly. Any proposition or plan projected must be demonstrable and implementable.

Nation development and growth depend on what the active populace can see.

There is need to see something that can make the thinking to understand the need to effect various consideration to be able to move ahead or forge ahead. Any nation that does not intend to be stagnated must never stop thinking. The nation thinks through the populace, and also manifests her thinking through them. Therefore, any nation that does not think well might never be able to resolve the whole lots of the issues that should be exterminated at the dispensation of operation. Major issue that confronts the African nations is not because the issues are enormous, but the issues that should have been resolved yesterday and today are always not resolved, but remain till the future issues are added to them. When issue is resting on issues, it becomes more tedious to have solution to them. Simple issues of today are difficult issues of tomorrow when there is no provision for them to be resolved.

Develoment of a society is strictly based on the prevailing education and exposure. When the education is lost, the future glory is doomed. When there is no adequate foresight to look into the need and the wants of the presence and the future, a conducive environment can not be attained. The citizenry must have something cogent that can be a contribution to the greatness of their environment. There must be need to see various projects and anticipation working for the benefit of the populace and the economy.

The world might not grow and advance without technology and expansion in reasoning. Let us look into the contribution of the technolonogy in whole. Many things can be done right away from where people are seated or standing across the world without moving an intch. Just got a new friend from oversea and we chat frequently! You can view people on your mobile lines while communicating with them, you may not border yourself with the purchase of the generator or electrification if you can afford solar energy electrification. Everything are computerized, there is almost provision for all the necessary information you require on the internet with or little stress. During the hot season, you might not even feel it at all if there is provision of viable and sorphisticated air conditioning. There is translation on the use of the machineries for farm use other than using of the crude and old tools and implements. Domestic animals that are meant for the consumption and other animals and products do not use their initial time period before they are riped or old enough to be eaten, and many more.

Education makes easiness to discovery and application of technology. If not because of the education and its application, it might be a bit tensed to get to the level at which we are as a world. The various discoveries and technology are made available and initiated by the concept of the education. The enlargement in the thinking faculty of the human had made them to think to the level at which they operate. Different kind of brain storming had brought about dissimilar issues that various individuals work on how to give remedy.

As a people, education is pertinent to create a suitable and conducive living. I have said this before now while I was analyzing on the impact of the education to the environment. The impact of the human is essential for the turn around and transformation they have. To have a good and thorough education that can reposition human, there must be sufficiency of education. Things that are needed for the immediate desire are different from those things that are meant for the future purpose, and these must be well alligned and analyzed with various yard sticks and measures that can give a genuine result to create conducive environment.

The state of mind has to do with the state of creativity. It means that, what you have in you or can access in your mind are the product of what you do. When you access something uncommon, there is every tendency to create things that are not common. Common sense is quite essential in coming forth with the reasonable outcome, and this can only surface through the work of the information. Out of the abundance of the heart comes out the inspiration that makes a life that one lives.

Education is the only security and escape route from the doom. When the information is well analysed and managed, there is always the need to be directed towards the path to the better end. There is always a better end when one can pave way for it. Sincerely, at the point at which arrangement is made, there might not be capital or financial surficiency around you, but the moment your projection attains the stage of maturity, it becomes the structure that allows you to erect your right choice and desired program.Through the presentation of what one has, industrilizaton are made available, vocational jobs are catered for, resources are mined and various testings are done to know how best they can be utilized, and so on.

Hence, the need to have a competitive and resounding education that can make nothing to be what the world can celebrate. There are many nations that in the last a decade, they were not noticed, but their discovery of the importance of their contribution to the existence and the entire world had made them. When one can come from no where to somewhere, and can create out the invisible consideration, he tends to know more than someone that has no clue on what to do. The sufficiency of the mind in line with the due interpretation of the demands of the world should form the basis of having an edge way over the others, and being to have a competitive economy.

CONTACTS

TOPE ADENIJI

MD TOP METHOD VENTURE ENTERPRISES

+234-803-718-4404 OR +234-808-093-5806

tophye@yahoo.com

LAGOS, NIGERIA. WEST AFRICA.

www.ingramcontent.com/pod-product-compliance
Lightning Source LLC
Chambersburg PA
CBHW020632220526
45464CB00001B/113